9-1-1,

Who Will

Answer

Your Call?

Kelly R. Rasmussen, ABD, ENP

Raskel Publishing
Charlotte, MI

9-1-1, Who Will Answer Your Call?

The opinions expressed in this manuscript are solely the opinions of the author and do not represent the opinions or thoughts of the publisher. The author represents and warrants that s/he either owns or has the legal right to publish all material in this book.

ISBN-13: 978-0-9825584-0-9
ISBN-10: 0-9825584-0-9

First published in 2009

Raskel Publishing, 224 S. Cochran Ave., Charlotte, MI 48813
www.RaskelPublishing.com

PRINTED IN THE UNITED STATES OF AMERICA

For all of you who answer the call.
The job at the console is more than a job; it is an existence, a being, a place, and a marker in time that holds the lives and memories of so many others.
For those of you who take the mundane mixed with the monotonous, and then the most amazing calls for service.
You hear the cries of the anguished, the hopes of the hurting, and the reality of a life that can be so cruel or so awesome in a matter of seconds. You listen with your whole being and apply the salve of comfort with your words.
You have been my colleagues, my coworkers, my subordinates, my employees and most of all my own weird set of friends when nobody else understood the humor.
Know that you matter most of all.

WHAT IS A TELECOMMUNICATOR?

"A Telecommunicator is a person who can assimilate logical information, sufficient to dispatch emergency assistance from almost incomprehensible data which is given by the uninformed, angry, drunk, traumatized, injured, ill, distraught or those who have little or no command of the English language. These special people must make these determinations of need in very narrow parameters of time -- they cannot make mistakes -- preservation of life and property depends upon their mental acumen, instincts and abilities!"

~ Author unknown

Other Titles by
Kelly R. Rasmussen

9-1-1 Matters
This inspirational and motivational CD helps move you beyond the negativity of work and home environments. This CD can help you recognize the person you want to become.

Women in Public Safety Leadership: 10 Tips to Get to the Top
This book shows you the fast track to advancement. You can take years on the "trial and error" path or you can learn to get on the fast track to advancement with Kelly's "trial and success" method.

Leadership: 10 Must Have Traits for Great Leaders to Reach the Top
Learn the 10 essential traits for great leaders to get to the top in their industry. Are you up for the challenge? This Ebook will show you the necessary traits to advance to the top of your industry as well as help you evaluate where you are currently along your path.

You may place your order online at
www.TheDoctor911.com

Contents

Acknowledgments

Thank you to everyone who always said to me that I could and should write a book about all of my stories. And to everyone who ever said to me upon learning what I did for a living, "Oh that sounds like a stressful job," yes, it is. Thanks for asking more.

Thank you to all of my colleagues in the industry. There is a need, a cry for help from the 9-1-1 industry that nobody is hearing. Keep your voices loud and strong. Help will come.

Thank you to Mom and Dad for keeping me grounded.

Most of all thank you to Michelle, who put up with all of the hurts and heartache, joys and exasperations of the job. You put up with the shift work, the idiosyncrasies of my shift partners, and you especially made it easy for me to do the job. You deserve the biggest and best kudos for all of your support over the decades.

Foreword

My first grade teacher, Miss Dow, taught me how powerful words can be. Teachers throughout my life reinforced the lesson she taught me when I was all of six years old.

I remember always teasing and being teased by a fellow first grader named Carl. He and I would routinely trade hurtful words. One day it came to a head. There I was in my little pink dress and my blond hair, Carl in his faded, hand-me-down, holey jeans. We went out to recess that morning and one thing led to another as usual. The playground was one of those fenced areas at the top of a hill. There was no grass any longer. The ground had been worn down to its earthen bareness where our swing set sat. I remember the carved-out grooves in the ground beneath the swings, for as kids do, we scraped our feet as we would swing back and forth, creating our own indentation in the earth's shell. Carl and I were fighting, once again, while rolling around on the ground under the swings, in and out of those dips, when I saw Carl rise up into the air. I saw his feet dangling and his eyes bugged out at me. I felt my own body being lifted up and could tell that my feet were no longer in touch with the soil. We were carried a short distance to the classroom, where Miss Dow quickly placed us in our seats. Recess ended for the class. Miss Dow went to the front of the room and proceeded to tell all of us the most magical words I have ever savored, pondered, and considered: "You can win wars with words." I do not remember anything else from that speech or that day. I was a six-year-old imaginative child who knew that words were the most powerful tool in my arsenal, my toolbox, my brain. I was going to figure out what this kind, elderly, phenomenal first grade teacher was talking about if it took the rest of my life.

This book is my personal recollection of events.
Names, locations, and circumstances have been changed to
protect the callers as well as the coworkers.

Introduction

More than twenty years ago both Kelly and I entered this field looking for work that was interesting as well as meaningful, not to mention something that paid the bills. Starting out as corrections officers/dispatchers and working our way up through the ranks, I don't think either of us ever imagined the paths this vocation would lead us up. Yes, I said up, because this has not been a journey down. And what an amazing journey it has been! Being a 9-1-1 operator offers more opportunities for courage, optimism, self-confidence, and career options than you can imagine, even though those benefits aren't mentioned in the recruiting material.

When candidates are asked during a job interview for a 9-1-1 operator, "Why do you want this job?" I think the most frequently given answer by a candidate is, "Because I want to help people." Once in the public safety field, helping attitudes can become negative with the steady diet of crisis and tragedy they are fed. After all, no one calls 9-1-1 because they are having a good day!

Kelly shows us that the opposite attitude can be the norm and there's always room for positive thinking and a reason to be grateful at the end of the shift. Some are funny, some are sad, and some are just plain odd, but no matter the reason, a 9-1-1 call is always important to the person who made it AND to the person who answers it. The ability to be of service to others is a gift that often gets overlooked, and you are about to be reminded not to overlook that gift.

Whether you are about to embark on a new career in 9-1-1, a

veteran in the field, or are simply interested in what happens in the world of 9-1-1, welcome to the 9-1-1 community! The challenges this profession presents to us are sometimes hard, frustrating, and quite frankly, even heartbreaking. The possibilities are boundless. Climb aboard and get ready for a great ride!

Harriet Miller-Brown, J.D., ENP
Michigan State 9-1-1 Administrator

PART I

"You can win wars with words."
Miss Isla Mae Dow, First Grade Teacher

Courage

"Sheriff's office," I answer the phone.

"I just came home and found my brother hung in the bathroom."

I start to shake and drop my pencil twice, so I insert a couple of uhs and ums.

I ask the caller, "OK, do you know for sure that he's dead?"

"Yes, we've been expecting this for some time. He's tried it before but never succeeded. He's got severe depression and a bunch of other mental illnesses, but the doctors just can't get his meds right." He painstakingly outlines his brother's medical history for me.

By now my hands are shaking. I desperately look at my partner, who has grabbed another phone and is helping that person. I realize I haven't even started typing the call into the computer, so I put my pencil down and try to start typing.

"Your name, sir, uh–huh, and your address, uh-huh, and what is your phone number?"

"Will help be coming soon?" he asks quietly.

"Oh yessir," I answer quickly while entering the information into the computer. A few feet away, my partner sees the call pop up on his screen. So I inform the caller like I learned, "My partner is toning the proper agencies as we speak."

"Okay then, I'll just wait for them to get here." He seems spent, so I begin to let him go.

"Sir, if you have any questions, please don't hesitate to call me back." I attempt to reassure him.

"Okay, thank you." He hangs up.

I ask my partner if I need to do anything else. He quickly answers "no" while he gets the ambulance on the phone and gives them the address of the suicide.

I take a couple more calls, mostly information about prisoners and what time visitation starts and whether or not they can bring items to the jailed prisoners.

I see the square emergency button on the phone light up again. I push it and answer the call.

"Sheriff's office."

"I, uh, yeah, ma'am, are you the one I, uh, called earlier? About my brother being hung in the bathroom?" He is stuttering now, and oddly different than before. Obviously he's not as in control of his emotions this time as he tells me more about his brother.

"I tried to, uh…" He coughs a couple of times as he struggles to talk. I use fillers and ask more questions.

"Are you okay? What happened? Are the medics there yet?"

He catches his breath. "I tried to cut him down, you know, in the shower, but I can't cut the rope, it's too hard, it's too…" He trails off.

I answer quickly because now I'm the one who has to be in control.

"Sir, it's okay, don't worry, don't do anything more, the medics and my deputy are almost there. They will help you. You don't have to do this. Just go to the door and watch for them. I'm sure you can almost hear their sirens by now."

"Okay, I'll go do that, I'll wait, I'm sorry."

He's so blown away by the shock of it all; I can tell that it's starting to hit him. He was so sure before and so confident that I just melted inside to hear all of his weakness as he begins to cry on the phone with me.

"It's okay, Tim, they're on the way, just hang in there and we'll be there soon to help. Just go wait by the door."

"Okay, I will, thank you for your help." He starts to sob as he disconnects the phone.

As I hang up the handset, I exclaim, "OH MY FREAKIN' GOD! I CANNOT BELIEVE IT!" I turn to my partner Joe and start to well up with tears myself. "I cannot believe it," I repeat.

"What? What's the matter?" Joe asks me.

"I can't believe I just did that." I am crying now, not hard, but in total disbelief.

"What did you do?" He's anxious now. Being the senior dispatcher in the room, it's his responsibility if I make mistakes. He is still technically my trainer.

"I just told that guy to 'hang in there' and he has just come home and found his brother hung in the shower." I feel devastated.

"It's okay." Joe exhales deeply and now faces me. "It's OKAY, he probably didn't hear it or catch that you said it. He was just glad that you were here for him." He squares himself in his chair and leans towards me like a father would a child. His brass on his uniform collar glints in the light.

I nod at him and ask, "You think so?"

"Sure, the guy was pretty much in shock on that callback, wasn't he?"

Joe is making sense after all. And I did help the guy. I got help rolling to him. And I bonded with him like I saw my other trainers do so many times.

After two weeks of being on the job and for the first time being on my own, I had figured I was ready to go. I watched the buttons on the phone light up and when one did, I knew to hit it and answer, "Sheriff's office."

I have answered tons of calls already for my first real time without a trainer sitting at my side overlooking and listening in to all of my calls. I just never imagined that my first shift on my own would entail some guy who came home and found his brother hung in the shower.

I turn to Joe and ask, "Is this it?"

"Pretty much," he answers.

Joe doesn't talk much. He doesn't have to. People talk to him. He turns around in his chair and resumes his "watch." He watches for the phone to ring, watches out the windows through the fenced wall that surrounds our protected wing of the jail. The dispatch center is off in a corner with a chain-link fence that keeps us "safe." Joe looks through to the traffic racing by on the water-soaked side street. He watches to see when another cruiser will pass by the window and ask for us to open the "sally port" garage doors of the jail receiving area. Joe also watches out for me, the new kid. His career depends on it.

This is how I began my career in public safety dispatch. I was outfitted like a sheriff's deputy and had my own pretend swearing in. The sergeant's hand waved up, down, and sideways while he said a few "hummeda-hummedas" and all I did was sign a paper saying I had no arrest powers and that being a deputy was in name only. I was very much the rookie, and very much willing to learn. Nobody told me it would be by the seat of my pants. I learned from others by way of "the buddy system," as we refer to it now. I remember being so nervous listening to my "trainer" take calls that I edged forward enough in my chair that it tipped forward and dumped me out, nearly causing me to biff my chin on the countertop. I caught myself on my hands and knees and my trainer caught my acrobatic act out of the corner of her eye. She never missed a beat or a word of encouragement to the caller. She kept her eyes on me and rolled them as if it was the most hilarious thing she had ever seen. All the while, she kept the caller calm while she typed line after line into the narrative of the call. I felt like such a dork. That was truly my introduction to the public safety communications world.

After a few more non-important calls, Joe takes a tough call that must have triggered something. He hangs up the phone kind of gruffly and looks over at me. Realizing I am studying his every syllable and every move, he asks me if I know anything about how to deal with stress. My eyes must have bugged out as I looked at him and answered, "No, why?"

"Well, let's have a little lesson before our relief gets here."

He stands up behind his chair and grabs the metro phone book. It's about three and a half inches thick, if not four. He holds onto it as if it is a mad cat twisting in the wind. He looks past me down to the end of our long, skinny dispatch room and says, "Watch and learn." He winds up by hauling back as far as he can hold the book without dropping it and throws it as hard as he can. The room is about forty paces long and the open path is as wide as one of extra-wide grocery aisles. Thud! He nails an open spot on the end wall perfectly.

I sit and listen for the phone with one ear and keep the other eye and ear on my partner, who seems a bit crazed now.

"C'mon, try it." He stares at me with his hands on his hips.

As if receiving a direct order, I jump up and retrieve the phone book. I stand beside him neatly and haul back as he did. Thank goodness the phones and radio are quiet. I still don't know how this will help.

"C'mon, get ready to heave." He is standing off to the side now, against the back of his chair, giving me orders. I throw with all my strength. It plops just before it hits the wall.

"Okay, that was a good warm-up. Now let's try it again." He retrieves the book and starts to show me how to hold it by the bound edge when the phone rings. I lean over and grab the phone and advise a lady of visiting hours for the jail. I get back in my place. He decides to show me how to throw it again. He winds up as before and with steady aim, he hurls the book to the end of the room. WHAM! It hits a bull's eye on the end wall, striking the alarm panel that covers the courtroom. This alarm box is set up so that if a judge or any of the court office personnel in any of the courtrooms or court offices has a situation, they just push the alarm button. Or so I'm told. I never thought the alarm box even worked...until now. There's a deafening, screaming noise combined with a strobe-type light swirling around the room, and as Murphy's law takes effect, an officer calls on the radio for information pertaining to the call he's on.

"You answer him, I'll reset the alarm," Joe commands as he heads to the panel. He flips switches, unscrews things, and tries everything he can think of. A jail guard passes through and asks if he unplugged the dang thing yet. Joe does and it goes quiet. It is so quiet that my ears are still pounding. Joe is looking pretty serious but less grumpy as he takes his seat.

"So—you learn anything today?"

"Yessir, I learned how to deal with stress." A smile tickles across my lips.

"Good, that's what you were supposed to learn." He sort of smiles, too.

This was my first lesson on how to handle stress. I never imagined this might be my only stress management class. It takes a lot of courage to do this job.

Patience

At the end of the first week on my own, I think I have a pretty good grip on taking phone calls and getting help going. Saturday afternoon, Betty and I wrap up an amazing shift of personal injury accidents, medicals, and other distress calls. I start to walk out and realize that I forgot to enter a call into the computer. My relief has already taken the chair and is answering a call. I turn to Sheila, who is the senior partner on this shift.

"Can you enter a call for me?"

"Yeah, I guess so, what is it?" Sheila looks perturbed. She's been in this business since time began. She tells stories of the former sheriff and his wife when they lived upstairs and the wife was the cook for the prisoners. I imagine something silly like an Andy Griffith show complete with Aunt Bea and Opie. Sheila makes it hard to fit in here. I don't think she does it on purpose. She doesn't take the job lightly. I guess that's a good thing because it keeps me on my toes. She has a way about her that sets me up to think that I am doing well, then she tells me how it should be done, at least according to her. I never know if I'm doing it right, doing enough, or if I will ever fit in. Sometimes I feel that she wants me to ask the right questions but I don't know the questions to ask yet. There just isn't any way to know how long I will be tortured and it's the unknowing that wears me down.

"It's just a shoplifter report," I tell her, "after the fact, nobody around, no witnesses, just see the clerk for a report." I puff my chest out and speak confidently using the lingo like I've learned.

"Where?" She isn't impressed with my rookie self.

"Oh—yeah, the Pantry Cupboard," I answer because I've covered all my bases.

"Which one?" She nails me.

"Uh, I, uh, I dunno. We have more than one in the county?" I ask as all the blood drains from my head.

"Duh, yeah, we have four in the county, but I'll call them all and see who it was that called," Sheila says with a huff and rips the paper from my hand.

"Okay, thanks." I think.

Being new wasn't so bad, but being new in this group of people was going to be a case of either make it or die trying. Maybe I should keep that metro phone book close by.

The next day, Joe shrugs it off when I ask him if I screwed up the day before. He tells me it takes a lot of guts to do this job.

"And what I see of you, you got good guts. Don't worry about it."

I like Joe, he's pretty cool. I might have good guts, but they sure get tied into knots when I push that button and answer the phone.

"Sheriff's office."

"Yeah, I want to know when someone is going to do something about all of these damn kids partying at the end of my cul-de-sac. I'm sick and tired of going down there every morning and picking up beer cans and cigarette butts. What the hell are you people doing about it?"

"Well, sir, can I have your name and address so I can see what—"

He cuts me off. "I shouldn't have to give you my name, you should know it by now. I call every Saturday and Sunday morning and you people never do anything about this. I want to know how to call and complain to the sheriff."

I get a little nervous that I haven't even begun to address his complaint and he already wants to complain to the sheriff. This can't be good. I try two more times to get a word in edgewise and

Joe sees and hears me struggling. I finally ask the man if he can hold the line and he keeps talking as I push the red hold button. I look at Joe for advice.

"Just tell him politely that we will add his cul-de-sac to the nightly patrols. We'll have the deputies post it at their branch office so they know to take a ride through there on Friday and Saturday nights."

I grin at Joe and tell him thanks, and push the blinking red button with confidence. I hear him still talking on the other end. I try to interrupt nicely.

"Sir…sir…uh sir…if I could…"

Now he's really mad that I interrupted him.

"Don't call me sir, and what the hell are you doing? You can't even give me a straight answer. I'm looking for the number for the sheriff, can you even come up with that? What's your name?"

He's on a roll now, and I still haven't followed through per the instructions of my senior partner, so I look over at Joe and he motions for me to put the caller on hold again. I do so quickly and Joe picks up the line from his desk.

"Sir, yes, I understand, okay then, John, what is it that you're after today? Yes, I see, okay, sure, yeah—I bet, okay...well John, as my lieutenant was telling you…"

I don't hear another word he says. When I caught that my partner just increased my rank by a couple of positions, I was amazed. My eyes must have popped out of the sockets because when I look over at Joe, he is smiling and nodding at the man's questions, then he winks at me. That wink taught me I could tame the world, and this job will definitely teach me patience.

Everything about the job is frightening but fun. It's like being on a roller-coaster. Most of the time you feel every click-clack of the track as you trudge up that hill. You look around you and everything seems normal with people going about their business. You look ahead again only to see the top of what seemed to be an insurmountable peak, only to crest it and shoot forward with speed and complexity that blows your hair back. The control is all about the power and determination. When you feel you can take back some of the control, the coaster takes a turn you didn't see coming and your stomach flips. It is the same in dispatch. I take the calls one after another and as soon as I think I know where the peak is and what is going to happen in the normal sequence, someone changes it up and I twist or turn upside down and wonder why the sky is green and the grass is blue. I build courage through each turn. I loosen my grip and open my eyes a little wider. I start to almost let my guard down when it screeches to a halt. So, I go again. This is the life of "answering the call." I can never get enough. And it challenges me every single time to a different degree.

Being on the job a few months raises my confidence. However, it was frightening to learn that after a mere six months, they were moving a road deputy into the senior chair as a "temporary assignment." And of all things, I had to train him. This was going to take more than an average amount of courage and patience. I smoked cigarettes. He didn't. That was the tip of the iceberg concerning our differences. He definitely made it clear that he didn't like being punished and sitting in that chair was the worst thing on earth to him. I couldn't imagine how we were going to get along.

Oddly enough, we started out okay. He was picking up on things that took me awhile to figure out. I didn't care for his phone demeanor though. He was rude and cocky and acted like the people calling were a burden to him personally. I tried to talk with him about it. He said I was "just a dispatcher" and he didn't have to listen to me. He was a cop and I wasn't enlightened as to what real police work was. Sitting here answering the phones was stupid and insignificant. This was the least and the greatest of our differences. I was gaining honor and respect with the job. He comes in and tries to tear it all down with his words. When that didn't work, he tried other things to break my spirit and exhibit his control. He "ordered" me to stop smoking because it bothered him. I smoked more. He got ruder with the callers, I begged him to cut it out. I felt like I was the senior dispatcher and he was going to get us both in trouble.

Finally, the day came. Not trouble like I thought, but good trouble in a sense. He placed the phone between his legs and defamed a caller. I walked over and pushed the hold button on his phone so I could pick up the extension from my end. He grabbed my arm and squeezed it tightly as he told me to stay out of his space. I jerked my arm away, which resulted in him standing toe to toe with me. Now—understand he was a tad shorter than me and this might have bothered him somewhat—he got closer to me and basically chest-butted me. I didn't know what came over me and with each of my hands on the epaulets of his uniform shirt, I pushed him backwards. He lost his balance and went down to the floor. Then he tripped me and soon we were both rolling around on the dirty floor throwing punches and swearing like sailors. As all of this was going on, the person on the phone hung up. I saw the light go out. And then someone called on the radio.

"Thirty-one to dispatch."

I reached the foot pedal with my hand and hollered up to the desk microphone and answered him.

"Go ahead."

"I'm clear of the last."

"I'm clear you're clear."

When my "favorite" deputy dispatcher started swearing again, calling me every name in the book, I merely reached over once again and pressed open the microphone with the foot pedal. His face went deep red. He let go. And I let go, of him and the foot pedal.

That was the best domestic I ever took in dispatch. As it turned out years later, I became good friends with Deputy Adamson. I had occasions to save his life when he returned to the road patrol and we both knew it was personal. As much as he ticked me off or ticked off my co-workers, they always knew that he and I had a special bond. I would look out for him because I knew the real him. We both grew a lot from that experience. Then we turned it in our favor to learn from it and grow together. But back when bad deputies were sent to dispatch as discipline, the fight was on. It was a fight for my territory, my philosophy, and for the love of my life. He learned it well. I could never imagine what his life was like in the patrol car, but I know that years later he confessed that after working that stint in dispatch, he gained a renewed respect for that department. I gained the courage to never allow anyone to disrespect the coolest job on earth ever again.

Deputy Adamson and I learned how to work with and for each other. We had to get to know each other's jobs and still be there for the caller on the other end of the phone, from afar. If anything, Deputy Adamson took some tough calls when he sat the chair. I remember the one he took from a scared father sobbing horrendously that he just ran over his child as she had been playing in the driveway. The daughter was the same age as Deputy Adamson's little girl at home. He made a connection. He must have visualized the weeping father on the other end of the phone holding his girl and pleading for help and feeling like he could die for his actions. This hard-core, ruthless, unprofessional deputy cried during and after that call. His eyes were opened after that. That's how I know he grew from the experience. In the end, Deputy Adamson learned the courage to do this remarkable job, and I learned a new patience to understand how tough things are from the road patrol point of view. Even more, I understood that an officer on the road does not always make a patient or even courageous dispatcher stuck behind a desk.

Compassion

The icky part of being a dispatcher/matron is the matron part. It is a throwback from the day when they didn't have any female guards, so they used matrons to pat down the female prisoners and take care of some of the female issues in the jail. I liken it to when the sheriff lived upstairs and perhaps the sheriff's wife or female relatives would overlook and handle the female inmates since they were few and far between. Since we are classified as "deputies" in the sheriff's department it is part of our job description. Our uniforms are the same as the road patrol, complete with the collar brass and the dorky female tie that crosses in front and snaps. At least we get to pick out our own black shoes or boots since we're technically not on the road or seen by anyone from the public. I guess it matters if I wear my uniform to work and home. I cannot disrespect the uniform while I am out in public. So I am careful to make sure that the woolen creases are accurately pressed and the brass is polished and shined and in the right positions. The collar brass was the most difficult to understand. The policy manual showed hand-drawn pictures. You would think I could get it right. But at least one shift a week, Joe would come over and adjust my brass. He was a military guy, so it makes me smile when, on occasion, I get it right and he looks over my uniform with approval.

The graveyard shift starts with a bang. I feel like I've taken three hundred loud music complaints and even more rowdy party complaints this hot July Friday night. Or maybe it just feels like that many. And that's just the first hour while the guy I'm relieving is trying to go home. I came in an hour early just to make his night so he could go home and have a little family time. Not likely now. He's grabbed another phone and it's a suicide threat. He writes S-U-I-C-I-D-E in big letters on a piece of scrap paper. Ted is our newbie. At least, he is newer than me. That's what matters most. I have seniority over someone! Right now none of that matters. Joe and I take call after call and the lights keep lighting, the phones keep ringing. Ted looks at me with that look—the look I must have had when I got my first tough suicide call of a hanging. I mouth the words to him, "For real?"

Ted nods his head in slow motion and mouths back to me, "*YES.*"

In between taking my own calls, I flip over the piece of paper and write a series of four questions to get him on a path with the caller. He cannot think of what to ask this lady who wants to kill herself. I pass him the note and hear him ask, "Okay Sally, what did you do or are going to do to end it?"

He looks at me as if to seek affirmation that that's what I really wanted him to ask. I didn't have time to fool around with her or him or anyone else. I wanted Joe to be able to handle the rest of the calls, so Ted and I could get through this one. I nodded at him and he continued.

"Sally—Sally, are you there? Are you with me still?" Ted's got a frightened look on his face, as she must have said something that he wasn't expecting. He covers the mouthpiece and says out loud to me, "I think she did it. I think she took that bottle of pills."

"What makes you think she's not faking it?"

"Her words are getting really thick and slow, and she's fading on me fast."

"Okay, hang on," I say to him and grab another phone.

As I listen to another "suspicious vehicle, possible kids partying" complaint, I scribble down some more questions for Ted. I want him to find her. We might not have much time and we need every angle we can pursue. I give him questions about her kids, and the kids' counselors or teachers and church members or clergy. While he works that path and thinks up some good questions on his own, I get Joe involved. I brief him quickly on what Ted has and what we have done so far. "But," I tell him, "We still don't have an address." Time seems to stand still for us, and in reality all of this takes place in a minute or two.

Rule number one. First and foremost, always get the location. It doesn't mean diddly if you know their name or can call them back if they've passed out. If you don't have their location—THE END. That's one thing everyone has taught me well. Almost too well as I sometimes interrupt callers in my zeal to get their location.

Ted is working her for more possible connections and my steadfast partner Joe is talking with Ma Bell on getting a trace on her phone. Meanwhile, Ted tells me that she is clearly distraught about this married man who now says he won't divorce his wife to be with her and her kids. As I listen in on the call from time to time to see if it spurs more questions to help Ted, I see the panic in his eyes. I think we both realize that we could lose this lady. The kids are away at a relative's. She has clearly done what she said she would do by taking the whole bottle of pills and is halfway through the bottle of vodka. She is nearly passed out and we still do not have a fixed address. I hope the phone company can work miracles. I answer another ringing line. Ted hands me a piece of paper. It is the name of the sister who has the children! She either slipped, or Ted got a little tricky with his questions. I quickly find information in the computer on her sister and call her. I explain to her who we are and she wants to know why we are calling her at midnight. I ask her sister's address and she wakes fully as she responds directly, "What has she done?"

"Nothing yet, ma'am. We have her on the phone and we would like her address immediately so we can help her further."

She rambles off the address quickly and I turn to Joe as he hands me a piece of paper with the same address. The phone company came through also. I look at him with questions all over my face. He waves me off and says he will call the next county and get them rolling. Luckily or unluckily, she called into our office and not her own sheriff's department. It's okay as long as we still have time. I write a note explaining it to Ted, and he nods with a sigh of relief. He steps up his questions and his direct commands to her. He is now rapid-firing stuff at her to keep her conscious. "Nice job," I mouth and give him the thumbs-up sign. He shrugs his shoulders and smiles a half smile.

I continue answering phones. Man, I shouldn't have drunk all of that coffee already. I've got to go pee and I can't see how or when. Then, Joe motions to me with a closed fist and thumb pointing up and back, as he's hanging up the phone.

"They need a matron in the back."

I groan. It's a feeling important, busy groan, but it is with guilt that I leave my partners in the trenches to pat down a female drunk. Ick!

I slip through the heavy metal doors with my jail door key and hear them slam behind me. The cavernous echoes of door slams are replaced immediately with drunks talking loudly and cops laughing and giving instructions. There are serious officers, and those who make the job fun. There are officers in brown uniforms and variations of blue uniforms, both light and dark. They have descended on the jail booking area with an array of intoxicated persons. Allegedly drunk or not, they reek of alcohol, puke, and urine. I will never know how people can do this to themselves weekend after weekend.

The guard takes me around to the area also known as the "Breathalyzer Machine" area where a female is attempting to blow on the stem of a white tube connected to a machine used to measure her blood alcohol. She is insistent that if she smokes a cigarette, it will calm her down enough to be able to comply and blow in this tube like the guard is asking. He denies her request and asks her to blow again. He urges her to keep blowing, keep blowing, keep blowing, so he can get a good read. After a few tries, he tells the arresting officer that he has a good enough sample and she can proceed to lockup. That's my cue to step in and take over. I have her face the wall with legs spread out wide, and arms spread-eagle gripping the cold cinder block wall. From the top of the collar of her shirt, I start at the mid back area and run my two thumbs around to the front of the shirt collar. Then I run my two hands along each arm, going out the full extension to the cuffs or sleeves and unfold them for contraband or weapons. Then I go around the front and lift the bra cups so if any drugs are hidden they fall out or make her react by trying to catch them. Once the top is complete, I have to insert two fingers of each hand into her waistband and run them around the woman's middle to make sure no other needles or knives are present. I proceed down one leg at a time, patting and squeezing, patting again up to the crotch and back down the other leg. Since they've relinquished their shoes and belts at the check in, that pretty much fulfills my part of a "pat-down." The first couple of times, I did like I was trained (complete with hand-drawn instructions and body areas outlined). It doesn't just feel awkward, it is alarming. After the first few, I became emboldened and asked about gloves and other safety concerns. It took awhile, but soon all of us had to don gloves and have guards or officers present upon doing a pat-down. Some of the dispatcher/matrons used to go back and do a pat-down and contraband items would fall out, which caused a struggle to ensue between the two women as to who was quicker to recover. I assist the officer in taking the woman to the holding cell.

As I escort her into the cage, she turns and looks into my eyes while I am backing out. "I only had two beers. I have kids. They're going to ask where I am when they wake up. I am not drunk. I don't deserve to be here."

I think about the people who have been in crashes already tonight with alcohol as a factor in one car or another. I think to myself, at least your kids will have a mom in the morning.

I return to my console and I am grateful that there seems to be a lull in the action. Joe says he just sent Ted out the door because he heard I was done and on my way back. Not bad. I come in an hour early to get Ted out and he stays over an extra hour and a half. It's going to be one of those crazy, full-moon nights.

Joe asks me, "By the way, did you take a call about a suspicious vehicle on Lake Drive?"

I don't remember which call was which prior to the pat-down, so I start looking through the computer.

"It won't be in there, I looked," Joe assures me.

"I could have sworn I heard you ask about a car over on the end of Lake Drive and you were asking for a description," he goes on. "But when the sarge asked me about it, I couldn't recall and told him I'd ask you when you got back."

I desperately search my mind and my desk for any note or call that might have been entered and Joe just wasn't seeing the same thing. I start searching my garbage. There are a lot of notes in there, mostly about Ted's suicide. TED'S SUICIDE?! I look on the back of the note with the questions I gave Ted. There it is. The car. Lake Drive. I had taken a vehicle description and even a suspect description. I give it to Joe and show him what I had written. He suggests I narrate the current computer incident and update the comments complete with my badge number. As I am entering the data Joe takes another call, and I look at what call he has entered at that location on Lake Drive that had so many deputies dispatched there. There was a K9 officer sent also because there had been an assault. It seems that my "suspicious vehicle, possible kids partying" was indeed a rapist who climbed the railing up to a second-story apartment and raped a woman who lived there. The neighbor who called in a suspicious vehicle thought it was odd that no cops ever showed up. He approached the sergeant on the scene and explained that he did make a call to the sheriff's department. This woman was mentally challenged and was not able to fight off her attacker. He broke her collar bone in the process of raping her. She called her mother to come over, and the mother called us for the ambulance and subsequent report. All the while I was patting down a drunk. My stomach does several flips. I think I am going to vomit right there at my console. I still have to pee. I ask Joe if I can run to the bathroom. I promise myself after a good, quick cry that I will make up for this. I will never let a caller down ever again. I will never make mistakes again. I have to find a way to make this right. If I still have a job. Frankly, I can't blame anyone but me if they do fire me. Besides all that, I must never forget this night. The woman who was raped will certainly never forget. I feel dirty. And guilty. And responsible. How could I have known? How could I have not? The suicide woman? She was saved. Her kids also have a mom the next day after her stomach was pumped. She was very close to accomplishing her task. The drunk woman could have easily killed herself or others on the road that night. The woman who was raped was most innocent of all. How could I let that happen?

Sheila tells me later that it wasn't my fault. I can't get it out of my head that it was. Sheila opens up a bit and starts to tell me about her experiences. I understand more now, why she is so hard on me. Her expectations are high because she has lived through some pretty tough calls as well. I respect that. She tells me about the guy who murdered an entire family. She tells me what it was like listening to him talk about it during the trial. His words still echo in her mind. She shivers and tells me more about why we learn from others' experiences as much as we can. We don't want to be the one making the mistakes if we can help it. We get back to "my call," as we refer to it now. We talk about passing notes, and she encourages me to try to get away from using a pad of paper at all because of things like this. Then Sheila walks me through some role-playing and other call intake scenarios. We do some refresher training on entering the call into the computer. It doesn't make the hurt go away, but it does make me focus on building up my skills. I even start to understand why Sheila can be so gruff at times. I might even like her, eventually.

I was tired a lot but still enjoying the JOB. It seems my dog and I were now sharing the same trouble sleeping. We seldom knew if it was okay to eat breakfast for dinner or dinner for breakfast. Life was definitely topsy turvy. Living alone was good but there was plenty of time to think about the calls. I know my trainers and partners told me I wasn't supposed to bring the job home. It was the most unusual thing I have ever known. People would ask me what I do for a living, and I would tell them whether I was at the hair salon or the movie store or any other place. I would light up with pride when someone would ask what kinds of calls I take. Then I couldn't remember a one. I would go blank. I could tell people about the mundane calls like barking dogs, or MDOPs (malicious destruction of property) calls. As usual, I could see that those accounts didn't hold their interest. They wanted to know the salacious details of people's lives and how I handled them. After some time I was very selective about who knew where I worked. I didn't want to tell them all of the details. I didn't understand why people did what they did on any given day; much less when they did stuff that resulted in a phone call to our office. So I wasn't prepared to tell anyone much of anything about the job. I was still too new.

There was so much to learn. I often felt like my head would implode at the end of a shift. This was OJT, on the job training. It felt good. It also made my brains feel like scrambled eggs most of the time. I tried to learn it all as fast as I could. That meant I would forget other common things and make silly mistakes. People in the industry call this the "glass is full" syndrome. It means you have absorbed as much as you can for now and need to take a break from inputting any more into your brain. I think this is good for trainers and trainees to acknowledge. Betty knew this and was taking a lot of the calls this night, as I was allowed to just "veg" and take the non-emergencies if need be. One of those lines rang and so I answered the phone with some trepidation.

"Sheriff's office."

"Is this the police?" A little old lady's voice was on the other end of the line. She was so serious I had to sit upright in my chair.

"No ma'am, this is the sheriff's office, but we dispatch for the police."

"Well, I don't want the sheriff's office, I want the police."

I start to ask her if she has an emergency and she painstakingly tells me that it's none of my business.

"Ma'am, I can dispatch the police to your house if you want me to."

"I don't want you to do any such thing! I want to know the number to the police!"

I start to sweat. My senior partner Betty looks over at me with interest. Betty is like Sheila but not as uptight. She can go with the flow. That's not to say that she isn't professional. All of my senior partners are as strict and professional as can be. They take no guff, they pull no punches, and they expect you to follow their lead at all times. They do not accept mediocrity. I cradle the phone in between my cheek and shoulder and put my palms up in the air with bewilderment.

"Are you going to give me the number to the police?"

"I'm trying, ma'am. I need to know where you live first." I consult the map and try to determine if she is in the city limits, or in the township for a sheriff's deputy response. Either way, I can have the correct officer call her and see what her issue is and determine if she needs a response in person, since she's not forthcoming with me.

Clearly she is not satisfied with my fumbling and figuring. My partner listens in on the call to try to see if she can help me.

I ask another question. "Ma'am, are you in the city or the township?"

"What does that matter?" She is even more frustrated with me now.

"I need to know this so I can have the appropriate department contact you."

"It's a local number, butthead," she growls at me with exasperation.

I ask her to repeat because I wasn't sure what I just heard. She says it again, only louder and clearer, "IT'S A LOCAL NUMBER, BUTTHEAD!"

That's all she wrote.

My partner Betty is roaring now. She quickly disconnects the phone line that she was listening in on. She is laughing so hard that as she rocks forward, she bounces upward and out of her chair before she falls out of it. She continues laughing and wiping tears of laughter from the corners of her eyes as she staggers around the room. She is holding her stomach with one hand and pointing at me with the other.

"She just called you a butthead!" As if I hadn't noticed.

I calmly ignore her and continue with the caller. I give the kind, elderly lady the number for the local police department after checking the duty board to make sure someone is checked out at the office. I then radio him to listen for the phone, as he is going to get a call shortly and I am unable to tell if the caller needs an immediate response or not.

She hangs up on me.

I stare at the receiver in my hand and my partner is still laughing so violently that she is holding herself up by leaning over on the back of her chair. Geesh. I'm glad I was here for her to call me.

Officer Hunt from the police department calls about fifteen minutes later.

"Did you take that last call?"

"Yeah, it was me," I tell him.

"You sure ticked off one of our fine citizens. Do you know what she called you?"

My partner is listening in, of course, on the phone call now.

"Let me guess—butthead?" I retort. He starts laughing out loud and agreeing the whole time.

It's going to be a long night. About three in the morning I am just about to nod off. How does that happen with three pots of coffee in me? I'll never know.

"Sheriff's office"

"There's a fight at the Right Bar. You better get someone here now 'cuz I think those guys comin' back have baseball bats with them now. The one guy tried to run us over as he left the parking lot."

"Slow down, sir. What's your name?"

Click. He hangs up.

I enter the call as a fight call. Betty dispatches a deputy right away and finds him a backup. After they get to the scene we get a request for a detective. Betty and I both look at each other while she gets the detective on the phone. He asks if he really needs to respond. She attempts to confirm it on the air and the deputy on scene says he has an attempted felonious assault. Betty looks at me with a question mark in her eyes. She tells the detective that he needs to go and hangs up. She looks at me and asks what happened. I tell her what the guy said.

"Oh."

"Did I screw up again?" I am now wide awake for sure.

"Well, if he said they used a vehicle, then that's potentially a felonious assault since they used the vehicle as a weapon."

"Crap."

I cannot believe this. I'm tired, but wired, and just when I think I've got a handle on this job, I do something stupid like this and let a suspect leave the scene without so much as a question about the vehicle description.

Betty talks with the detective after the fact and tells me not to worry.

"It's okay, everyone at the bar knows who the guy was, so they have the suspect information."

I tell her I can't believe how much I can screw up before I get this job right.

"You'll never know it all. That's one thing I can tell you for sure. If you ever think you know it all you'd better get out of the business because you will get someone killed with that kind of thinking. That's the dangerous stuff."

I nod as if I understand. All I know tonight is that I'm a butthead and I need to find strength and compassion from the little calls. And that is some powerful OJT.

Strength

On my days off I hang out with friends and family. I listen to the scanner and hear the familiar voices on the radio. I run my dog and count the hours until I go back to work. I bike to the beach, and at the end of the day on my way home, I stop in at dispatch to see if they want an elephant ear or something from the carnival that's in town. While I am in visiting, they get a call of a bad crash on the drawbridge. That's not good. It closes down the whole southbound side of the bridge. Now there are boats that can't get back from the lake to the harbor because the bridge-tender cannot raise the bridge. The ambulances and rescue folks have to access the accident from the northbound lane and jump the middle barrier to access the victims. This means that the northbound traffic is reduced to one lane. Wow—what a mess. I jump in a chair and take a call.

"Sheriff's office"

"Please help me; oh please help me find my daughter."

"How may I help you, ma'am? What is your location?"

"Two-two-two E. Shelton, here in Grand City. My daughter, she's fifteen physically, but mentally she's about four years old. Please help me find her."

"How long has she been missing?"

"I thought she had gone to bed at nine but I just checked in on her and she is nowhere in the house."

I go through the motions of getting her name and physical descriptors and ask the mom about medications and places of interest. I get the call entered quickly and Betty looks over at me as if to say, "Good job, kid." She gets the call dispatched as a BOL or a "be on the lookout" for this missing child. Before there was an "Amber alert" or "a child is missing," the BOL was broadcast to everyone we thought necessary. We put the information out every way possible.

And in this case, Betty says out loud, "Dang it, I'm going to announce this to all those fire dudes and ambulance folks in case they see her standing around looking at all those lights."

She broadcasts the BOL again on fire and EMS frequencies. Unusual? Yes. Procedural? Nope. It was worth a shot.

The accident is a fatal. Dang. During the fireworks and commotion with the carnival and festival, there's a lot going on and this triples the call load. I ask Betty if she'd like me to stay. After some hesitation she admits it would be nice but that things should settle down in a little bit. She confirms that I'm going home so if it really hits the fan, she'll call me back in.

"Sure—you've got my number."

I get on my bike and skip the elephant ears. Once home, I hug my dog and tell her how lucky we are. She knows nothing I speak of. She only hears her name, "blah blah blah," "treat," and her name again. We both settle in for a little treat and some television.

The next morning I read the paper to see what the news is. What happened at the crash for real? What happened to the missing child? How did the carnival go? What other things made the news? And most of all, what did my partners have to go through the rest of the night? What types of calls did they take that nobody knows about? Were there any more suicides? Were there Domestics? How many Assaults? I read the paper and see nothing. There is a photo of the crash. I hope they notified all of the family before they read their morning paper.

I go in early for my afternoon shift. I figure it will allow me to catch up a little bit.

"Hi Sarge." I address my communications sergeant.

"I heard you stopped in for some overtime last night." He stares at me.

I stop in my tracks.

"Yessir, well, I uh, stopped by. I was uh, on my bike passing by and thought I'd see if anyone needed anything and they were really busy so I thought I'd help by grabbing a phone." I stammer like a fool.

"Well, was it authorized?"

I'm dumbfounded.

"Sir?"

"Was the overtime authorized?"

"Uh, well, it doesn't matter if it wasn't, you don't have to pay me, and I was on my own time…"

He puts his hand up to stop me as if I just stepped in a pile of poop.

"It's okay, kid, I was just teasin' you. It was a good thing you did. Just don't make a habit of it. You'll burn out quick like that."

"Yessir." I agree with him in spirit, but not deep in my heart.

"Sir?" I ask before he leaves my presence.

"Yes, rookie?"

"Did they find the missing fifteen-year-old last night?"

"Yeah—they did, out on the bridge watching the ambulance lights like Betty thought."

"Cool!"

I go get changed into my uniform and get prepared to start my shift. The afternoon shifts can fly by when you mix the summer heat with all of the bodies of water nearby. My first call is a road rage call. As I look back on it now, it is humorous that people would be so upset with road incidents that they would continue home and still call us with the details a good half hour after the incident. It is even more difficult to explain that the deputy didn't see the incident and couldn't really go after the person on that license plate, because there was no evidence as to who was driving. But still they call.

"Sheriff's office."

"I want to complain about some jerk on the highway. He was driving like a madman and he's going to get somebody killed."

"I see, and where did this happen, ma'am?" I am inquisitive.

"On Highway 32 as I was coming home tonight. He was in a red Chevy Camaro with a license plate of 'K' as in Kevin, 'W' as in wood, 'T' as in tree, '1', '2,' '3'."

I chuckle to myself. It took me a day and a half to memorize the phonetic alphabet. Now that I know it, it sounds strange when people make up their own words for the various letters. It is most fun when drunks call in to report other drunks and they make up letters like 'B' as in beer. I smile.

"Okay, so what did this guy do to make you so upset tonight?"

"He was up my rear end so far, I couldn't see his headlights. That's what makes me upset. He's going to get someone killed driving like that." She repeats how serious it is.

"Okay, were you in the driving lane or the passing lane?" I ask just as a matter of fact.

"What does it matter? If you must know, I was in the passing lane."

"Was there traffic in the driving lane, ma'am?"

"Well, NO, but I always drive in the passing lane, it is clearer."

"I see." I pause to let this idea sink into my brain, and perhaps into hers.

"But that shouldn't matter. He was driving in a very unsafe manner and I want him reported!"

"Okay, ma'am, I understand. I will take your information and turn it over to a deputy. I also want you to promise me that you will drive in the driving lane from now on unless you are passing another vehicle."

"Well, I guess I could try that," she admits begrudgingly.

"It's only for your continued safety that I ask this of you. And for you agreeing, I will pass along your information to a deputy."

"Okay, then," she agrees.

"I thank you for calling." I hang up and look at my partner.

"Well, I'm a deputy right?"

He agrees and I wad up the piece of paper and toss it into the garbage can.

Sometimes knowing what battles to fight is just as important as knowing if it is a battle or not to begin with. At this stage in the training and in the profession, we could still "screen" the calls. We know that something like this would not be handled by a road patrol officer and we were trained how to toss it. I know that training while sitting the chair isn't formal or anything, but I can feel that I'm starting to get it. I can tell which battles to engage in. I can feel the caller's voice and I can tell if they need me, and how desperately.

"Sheriff's office."

"I want an officer to come over here and make my daughter see how stupid she's acting."

"Okay, ma'am, let me see if I can do that for you. In the meantime, give me a little information if you would; your address? Okay, and how about a phone number? And who am I speaking with?"

"I'm her mother."

"I figured that much out. How about telling me your name and her name, please?"

"Oh yeah, I'm Martha and she's Kelly. She's fifteen and thinks she can run this house but I've got a few things she can think about. Like going to a foster home or somewhere. Somewhere they don't want you and treat you like shit. That's where she can go."

"Pretty powerful words coming from a mom." I slip in a statement.

"Well, that's how mad she's made me. She makes me want to send her away and make her grow up in a place where it's a hell of a lot harder than here. She don't know how good she's got it. When I was growin' up if I talked to my mother like she talks to me, I'd get a smack across the mouth. BUT not nowadays. Them teachers will report you quicker than snot that you abuse your kid, then you're in deep shit. Well I ain't hittin' nobody but she sure as hell better start minding me. That's why I want a cop over here. I want them to tell her how the real world is and what they do to fifteen-year-old girls on the street."

"Martha?" I gently ask.

"Yes." She takes a breath.

"May I speak to Kelly?"

"Yeah sure, see if you can talk any sense into her....Here, take the goddamn phone. She wants to talk to you. I don't know what about, just come get the phone. Get over here right now and talk to this lady or ELSE!"

"Hello?" I hear a tight-lipped female teen take the phone from her mom.

"Are you Kelly?"

"Yeah, who wants to know?"

"I do. My name is Kelly too."

"So, what do you want?"

"Well, Kelly, I want to help you and your mom get along better tonight."

"Why? It won't fuckin' help. She's too fucking controlling."

In the background I hear Mom yelling at Kelly to watch her mouth.

"Well, it's true."

"I understand how moms can be." I try to build a bond with her.

"So—are you a mom or something?"

"Uh—no, but I had one. Does that count? I had a mom and I was fifteen once. Right?"

"Oh, yeah, whatever. I bet your mom didn't try to control your whole freakin' life tellin' you who you could hang out with and who you couldn't."

"Oh yes she did. She did it a lot!"

"Didn't it piss you off?"

"Yeah, sure. But she never called the cops on me."

"So you sending a cop over here to yell at me?"

"No, that's why I'm taking a few minutes to talk with you

myself. I have to be honest, Kelly, all of my officers are tied up. We had a very serious shooting in an area of the county that it pulled all of my officers who normally patrol your area. So it's going to be awhile before anyone is free."

"Wow, that's too bad. Who got shot?"

"Some guy. They think he was an innocent dude who was in the wrong place at the wrong time."

"That sucks."

"Yeah, life is pretty dang short, huh?"

"Yeah, tell my mom that so she'll get off my case."

"Well, Kelly, I can tell her that if you want me to. But can I explain to you first why she's on your case?"

"How do you know?"

"Easy, I work here. I see kids all the time getting into trouble. I dispatch lots of police and ambulances to kids killed in rollover crashes with or without alcohol. I hear stories of moms filing runaway reports by the dozens. They cry on the phone because they think they will never see their kid again. They would take it all back if they could, if only they could hug their kid once more. Some do, some never get the chance. They have to identify the body at the morgue."

"Wow, that would suck."

"Yeah, imagine your mom looking over your body on some slab of concrete. Think how hard she would be taking it because she wishes you would have just listened to her that one time. Man—she would hate herself forever, huh?"

"Yeah, I guess so."

"That's what she's doing now. She knows you will hate her a ton right now, but she would rather live with that than hating herself for not stepping in if something happened to you."

"Well, if she would only listen to me."

"I can help maybe? Would you like to get your mom on the other phone and talk together?"

"Will you talk to her like you talked to me just now?"

"Sure, Kelly, I will keep talking if it keeps you and your mom together. Remember, I have a mom too. I don't talk to her anymore. So maybe I can make it up by helping you and your mom."

We talk for the next twenty-five minutes. The three of us. We just talk and laugh and cry a little. We share mother and daughter struggles. I fill in the gaps of what happens when the communication breaks down. They thank me and they say they will try to work things out tonight. They ask if they can cancel the call for police response.

"What call?" I ask.

They smile on the phone; I can hear it from each of them. I thank them for listening. In turn, they thank me for being here. I tell them to call again if they ever need to, but remember to try to talk with each other first. Mostly, I remind them to listen to one another.

"What a freakin' counseling call that was, huh?" Sheila looks at me in the eye as I wipe the remainder of a tear.

"Yeah. Counselor, social worker, investigator—we do it all, huh?"

"Yep, kid, and don't you forget it. Now get back to work."

I cannot imagine my own mother calling the police on an argument between us. We probably should have once or twice to get some cooling down time. Life's lessons are hard, but boy do they come in handy. I imagine Joe would have handled that call totally different. Maybe it was meant to be that Martha and Kelly got me tonight. I don't necessarily believe in fate or stuff like that, but I believe that answering this phone night after night will teach me things I could never learn anywhere else. I get stronger with every call.

"Sheriff's office."
"What time do they do the fireworks tonight?"
"At dark."
"When is that?"

"Sheriff's office."

"Is the bridge open?"

"No, if it was, all of the cars would fall in the water."

"Sheriff's office."

"Can you tell me what the road conditions are?"

"Hard and black."

"Sheriff's office."

"What is the weather doing in Milton?" (Thirty miles from my window.)

"I really couldn't tell you."

"Sheriff's office."

"Should I go in to work tonight or are the roads too snowy?"

"Give your notice."

"Sheriff's office."

"Your mama eats refried beans and farts."

"Excuse me?"

Click.

Sometimes we want to be a smart aleck to people and give smart aleck answers to dumb questions. But we don't. We try our best to give non-incriminating answers that remove our liability. We tell people approximately what time dark is because it takes too long to tell them to dial a non-emergency number. We tell people that the drawbridge is functioning normally and traffic is fine. We tell them that snow on the roads means "normal winter driving conditions." Which translates to "if you know how to drive in the winter, go ahead, go slow and be cautious as usual." If you are visiting here or have never driven in winter, stay the heck home. Especially if you need to travel thirty miles away in the dark, snowy winter. If you feel you should not go to work, call your boss and ask him. Mostly, if you want to talk about my mama, have the guts to stay on the line until I can get a trace on the call and have some cop roll up to the phone booth and smack the snot out of you for wasting my time.

Okay—enough of the silly stuff. But really, this is what builds strength. It adds to the diversity of the job. It is the OJT that makes you practice being nice to every caller. I will never forget taking call after call from some snotty-nosed kid who kept calling and blowing raspberries. How I would have given anything to have E-9-1-1 back then so I could tell where he was calling from.

"Sheriff's office."

"Ppppsbbbsllltt." Click.

"Sheriff's office."

"Ppppsbbbsllltt." Click.

"Sheriff's office, if you do not have an emergency, you are tying up an emergency line," I rattle off in rapid succession, trying to guilt the little bugger.

"Ppppsbbbsllltt." Click.

Golldangit! I'll get him this time, I'm thinking.

"Sheriff's office, I am sending the police. They are on the way to your location now!"

"Oh good dear, my husband, he not feel so good. Please come! We have no phone, so I come to the corner store to call. Please come, I wait right here."

"UH-OK-UM-YEAH, what is your name, ma'am?"

Damn kids. Good thing I didn't cuss him out this time. Strength builds character. I think I will need it.

Faith

Wherever you go, whatever you do, there are two kinds of people on this planet—those who believe in UFOs (unidentified flying objects) and those who think you are nutso if you subscribe to that theory. We actually made the national news with the numerous reports of sightings in the area. I swear that after listening to call after call one night, the people truly saw what they saw. I could never understand what they wanted us to do about it, but still the calls came repeatedly.

"Sheriff's office."

"There's a bright light out in the sky to the northwest. I think you folks need to check it out."

"Okay, what kind of light, sir?"

"The thing is weird. It sits still for a while, then moves like in a diagonal direction, then back across the sky and back to its original place. It's sittin' there right now. I think you should send an officer down here to check it out. We've seen it out over the lake before, but tonight it acts more like it's watching us."

"I see, sir. So I take it that it's not a plane or helicopter about to crash, or even some spotlight from some store opening somewhere, right?

"You got it. It's a damn UFO if I ever saw one, and I don't believe in that crap."

"Okay, I gotcha, I will send a deputy through the area and see what he can see. Do you want him to stop and speak with you?"

"No, that ain't necessary. I just thought you people need to check this out, thanks."

"Thank you, sir."

"Car 32, copy a suspicious."

"Car 32, go ahead."

"Check out a suspicious light in the sky to the northeast of the area of Lakeshore and Tannel drives."

"Uh—dispatch—a light in the sky?"

"Affirmative, caller doesn't wish to be seen, but we have had several calls and many of them concerned enough to ask for someone to check it out."

"Car 32 clear and en route."

"Okay, be sure to advise us what you find."

"Click, click, click-click, click, click-click-click" go the microphones. Everyone out there who is listening is clicking their microphones as a form of laughing this time. They love it that this deputy just got dispatched to a UFO call. They are all saying to themselves that they're glad it wasn't them. But secretly, a few of them close by the area are sliding down that way to see what they can see as well. Curiosity. After about fifteen minutes, I hear from the deputy.

"Car 32 to dispatch…"

"Go ahead, car 32."

"There's a light in the sky confirmed."

I'm stumped. I look over at my partner Betty and wishing Joe was here tonight for this one. She shrugs at me as if to say, "You asked him to check it and advise."

"Car 32, I am clear there is a light. I will advise the remaining callers that we have checked it out."

"Uh, dispatch. You can tell them I agree. It's pretty freakin' weird."

GASP! Betty looks over at me like I just yelled in the ear of every media person in a hundred-mile vicinity.

"Clear car 32."

"Thirty-two dispatch, I'll be in the area awhile. Some of the callers have come out to talk with me."

Oh my gosh. I never would have imagined it would be this crazy. I just wanted a deputy to go look and say yep or nope, it's a light and be done with it.

This could balloon into something ugly. My partner is already fielding calls from more deputies and other officers. She's laughing with me this time, not at me…I hope.

Car 32 calls me on the phone after another hour drags by.

"Kelly, did you take the calls from these folks down here?"

I am cautious to answer. I don't know if I am in trouble again or not. Was this a cop thing, was it really something to send deputies to or not? Is he going to instruct me on the law like the difference between a felony and misdemeanor or more like a police UFO versus a non-police UFO? Who makes these rules? And how am I supposed to remember them all?

"Uh, yeah. I got a ton of calls. They all sounded pretty scared. Why?"

"I can see why. I've been watching this thing for an hour and it's pretty freakin' scary. I talked to several of the callers. They said they had bets about whether I would show up. They said it made them feel better that I came. As much as I don't like this crap, and I am gettin' the hell out of here now, ya done good! But I'm not comin' back out here. Give it to 31 if ya need. He drove out here, saw it, and took off."

I laugh with him nervously and we both talk about how this light has captivated everyone. We decide to call it a night concerning this call. We hope!

Life is definitely weird enough when it's just you or you and your circle of family and friends. It can even be a little weird with your worker family, but when that family deals with the morbid truths of everyone else's lives, it is over a hundred gazillion times weirder. The stories are beyond belief sometimes. People do amazing things to one another. None of it makes sense. And try as we might to prevent things from happening, we are usually on the other end that concerns cleaning up the messes. We get good at it because we are cynical. We have a saying in dispatch: "In God we trust, all others we run through LEIN (Law Enforcement Information Network)," the local law enforcement information computer that checks people and plates for warrants or other outstanding issues. We become cautious, cynical, skeptical, and critical of all people. We "see" things on the phone. Most of the time we imagine it ten times worse than what the reality is, but it does make you wonder how one can live with all of that cynicism and skepticism.

As I sit looking at the outdoor cameras trained on the jail entry and exit doors one snowy night, I ask Betty what the blob is in the bottom left camera view. She stands up and walks over to the camera and says, "I dunno, looks like a garbage bag got dumped at the bottom of the stairs."

"Should I go check it out?"

"Sure, kid, you go, I'll hold down the phones." (There hasn't been a phone call in the last two hours other than calls from the officers.)

"Are you sure? I mean, what if it's a plot or a scam?" I'm a little nervous.

"Just go. Or not. Or tell the guards. It's their area," she says hurriedly and goes back to reading her book.

"That's a good idea, I'll call back there."

"Shepard." Corrections officer Matt Shepard answers the phone quickly and curtly.

"Hey, you guys have a bag of garbage or somethin' at the bottom of the front door stairwell, can you check it out?" I ask him in a rattled but quick fashion.

"No Kel, can you get it for us, we're swampin' busy from a fight and have to move a bunch of folks from cell to cell."

"Well, all right then."

Click.

"What'd they say?" asks Betty.

"They're busy."

I stand and move close to the camera to see if I can figure out what the shape is. I'm more baffled than nervous now.

"Okay, I'm going up and out but I'm taking a portable so I can yell if it's a ploy to break in." (As ironic as it sounded, I thought people might try to fake it to get into the jail to be with their loved ones.)

"Yeah, okay, kid, whatever you say. I'm here for ya."

I go upstairs and open the first wooden door to the lobby. I let it lock softly behind me. I have the only key between me and what's outside and I can't leave the door propped open and endanger all of my coworkers. I open the outside door cautiously. I peer down the snow-dusted stairwell. There are no fresh tracks. I start to step down the first stair and the object moves. IT'S THE JAIL COOK!

I buzz the intercom buzzer on the outside of the front door and Betty answers.

"You playin' in the snow or what?"

"I need an ambulance. The cook is down at the bottom of the stairs. I don't know how bad, but there's no fresh tracks or anything." I'm stammering, so I have to remind myself to let go of the button for Betty to answer me back.

Betty responds, "I got the ambulance on the phone and the city is sending the cavalry."

She's going to be okay. Within seconds of letting go of the buzzer my partner Betty did have an officer on scene with me. Maybe Betty sent him to begin with, to help me in case it wasn't a garbage bag. I don't know. He gets there and stands over the object who is now a person. He looks up at me frozen in place, still having one foot on each of the top two steps.

"Go in and tell Betty we've got a bad fall here." His words jolt me back to reality.

"Okay." I must have looked pretty dazed because he gives me orders without so much as a "hello" or a "how-ya-doin', Kel."

I run inside, fumble with my key at the second door, and go tell Betty. She looks at me quizzically at first. I repeat what the officer said. "The jail cook took a bad fall. She's lying in a heap at the bottom of the stairs."

"Oh—okay," she says out loud.

I can see her processing what I just told her and her brain immediately kicks into gear.

I hear her calling the jail lieutenant at home to inform him of the employee down. Then she calls the guards in back for salt and shovels per the lieutenant's instructions. They respond immediately to the front stairs. We watch them on the video cameras as they salt the bare patch of concrete where the cook had been lying.

Betty looks over at me and I look at her.

"Well, that made the night fly, huh?" I ask.

"Yeah, good thing you were checking the cameras."

We both wonder aloud about how long she was at the bottom of the stairs and what might have happened if I hadn't gone to check. We don't want to go there.

The guards check in with us later on that morning. They advise that the cook is going to be okay and they remind us that the steps are salted. They ask if I went down to check on the cook when I found her.

"Uh, no, I didn't think about that. It was my first body. I wasn't about to be ambushed if they were fakin'."

They all laugh out loud, at me, this time.

There are nights where I feel the clock has frozen in place. This is one of those nights. After last night's body in the stairwell, who knows how we will pass the time tonight. (In retrospect, these were the best of times because we never knew how busy and how much more advanced answering the call was becoming.) We ask the guards how things are going in the back and they are pretty quiet too. One of them sits at the booking desk and the other two come visit us in dispatch. We grab cards, the cribbage board, or whatever we feel at the moment and play the night away. Pot after pot of black coffee disappears. Sheila is the dealer for this hand of euchre. I grab a lonely phone call. It's an OUIL (operating under the influence of liquor) report, after the fact, of course. Someone drove all the way home and called it in. I enter the call and Sheila keys up the microphone to broadcast the BOL. These are the days of no headsets yet, so I watch as she reads and talks over the air without any nervousness. She's always so cool, so fluid. Then I see her do something I would never imagine. She shuffles the deck of cards in anticipation of our next hand. She raps the cards solidly on the desk, and rat-a-tat shuffle-pbbbllpp over and over. I am frozen in my tracks yet again, this time in my mind. I walk over cautiously and put my hand on her hand and she stops shuffling but continues reading the vehicle description and plate information, and looks up at me with her eyes totally bugged out. She releases the microphone and we both start laughing. Click-click-click go the mics. The guys on the road know that we've been passing the time with a deck of cards at least. Now we are laughing so hard that we are holding our stomachs.

She runs to the women's locker room screaming, "I'm going to pee my pants."

The jail guards sit among us shaking their heads.

"Is this what you guys do for fun?"

"Sure, we are trained professionals." It is a tag line we all use to sum up anything. Being professional to us means believing in people, no matter what. We have faith in each other, the job, and the fact that it is the coolest job in the world. We just had no idea how many changes were in store for us.

The next day I worked afternoon shift. Usually, I work just about whenever anyone needs me to. I blend from one eight hour into the next. This afternoon we are bombarded with domestics, larcenies, fights, drunks, and the ordinary, everyday types of calls. The calls that are the toughest always involve children. The next one does just that. It is a transfer from the city dispatcher who sits in her little dispatch room a few blocks away.

"Sheriff's office."

"Hey Kel, it's Laurie, I've got a bad one for you. It's a guy who was target shooting outside and left his kids outside while he took a phone call. Kid picked up gun and shot little brother. Copy the address and phone number."

I go blank. My heart stops pumping. I feel all of my blood dump out at my toes. My hands go cold and my fingers numb. It is hard to focus on writing everything down. I thank her for the call and hang up. I enter it into the computer in seconds and look over at my partner while I pick up the phone to dial the number to the residence in question. In those days, we never had any training on medical dispatch. There was no such thing. It was just a simple statement that we were on the way and hang up. We didn't encourage follow-through. It invited liability or something. But I had to make sure they were still there at the scene. I had to make sure they knew we were coming. I had to reach out to this family.

"HELLO! Help us!" a woman shouted on the phone as she picked up.

"Ma'am this is the sheriff's office and we are sending the ambulance and deputies to help you. Can you tell me what happened?"

"My baby, oh my baby, oh my GOD! My husband, came in, oh my god, only for a second, and took a phone call. We heard the shot..." Heavy sobs and gasps for air. I hear the anguished father in the background, "Ohhhhhhhhhhh please God no-o-o-o-o-o-o-o." The guttural pleading falls on deaf ears. And mine. It is difficult to decide what to do next. I look at my partner for help. Nothing. Sometimes you just pull the words out of the bottom of your heart and you speak to their heart. I lower my voice in communion with the grieving mother.

"Ma'am, we are sending help."

"Oh god no-o-o-o-o-o-o, there's no help. He's not breathing. He's DEAD!" She drags out the word with wailing.

Then, there are no words. Only silence. There is only agonized breathing, tormented wails, and the terror of holding their dead child. Again, the guttural cries of anguish are that of some alien sound that must be in a pitch that others aren't supposed to hear. They cannot hear how they sound. I cannot fully describe the intensity of the pain and yet I feel as if I am conjoined with them. Our bodies and spirits share one moment in time as real as if I am standing half inside of them, half beside them.

I hear the medics arrive on scene and the phone disconnects.

I call the city dispatcher.

"Hey Laurie, it's Kelly."

"You okay, kid?"

"Not really, but I don't really know how to be." I am numb but I ask her more. "What did you get for details? I really don't know much more. I didn't have a chance to ask much."

"Yeah, that pretty much describes it. I got the mom at first yelling at me to hurry and get there because they were being told by the older kid that he just shot the younger one. By the time mom gives me the address and stuff, the dad's racing into the house carrying the dead kid in his arms." Laurie takes a deep breath in and exhales slowly.

"Shit." (I am imagining the scene in my head. I see the mom, the dad, the dead child in his arms.)

"Yeah, tell me about it. I'm glad it was yours and not ours." Laurie is trying to joke it off.

"I'm sure we'll get even. I'll dream up a floater for ya if you want."

That's the way of describing a dead body in the water. I try to make light of one tragedy with another that is hopefully make-believe. Only in the real world, we all know the likelihood of it is all too possible.

"Yeah, but hopefully I won't be working."

"Yeah, whatever, thanks, Laur."

"You're welcome, kid…I think."

I think this job can be very sad, very scary, and very sucky. This is one of those days, and it can test anyone's faith in anything.

PART II

The time came when we needed to make a change. The sheriff's department was no longer going to be in charge of the dispatch center. I have to choose to either go back into the jail and become a corrections officer, or take a chance and go to the newly formed 9-1-1 center and see what happened. It is all so uncertain. Five years of learning the ropes and taking the call and now they want me to figure out if I will fit in at this new 9-1-1 dispatch center. I like the idea of knowing where the calls are coming from with this enhanced 9-1-1 idea. I like the idea of a new building (well, a remodeled basement won't be bad). We will have new equipment and a locker room and a kitchen area for breaks. It's tough to compare all of that to the patting down of sloppy drunks for the rest of my career. I know there is so much more to being a corrections officer, and believe me, I think they have to have many personalities of their own in order to survive in that arena. It just isn't as enticing to me as doing this phenomenal job of answering the call. My decision is made. I move with the center.

Fear

It is scary walking into that first training session with the new CAD (computer-aided dispatch) and being told we would learn to leave our pens and paper behind. Everything is entered into the new CAD and it will recommend units for dispatch to send and it will keep a history of all of our records entered. The merger brought the "city" dispatchers together with those of us from the "county." We've talked with them for years on the phone exchanging calls that belonged in each other's jurisdictions. We know their voices, have shared their pain and laughed at the silly things together. Still, now, we are told we will all have to work side by side and teach each other all that we know. It is training by symbiosis. As successful as we are, there are plenty of bumps along the way. And keep in mind that there still was no formal training of any sort. We learn by watching, asking, sharing, and, painfully sometimes, by experience. The calls never stop. It's just that now we can tell more easily where they come from.

"9-1-1."

"Yes, I would like to know when the parade starts and I cannot find the local number for the police department anymore. Can you tell me?"

"Um, yes ma'am but for future would you please call our non-emergency phone number?"

"Of course. If I remember it next time."

Such is the re-education process. Now we hear from every city, township, and locale for all types of information being sought.

Strangely enough, I don't miss those pat-downs back in booking.

"9-1-1."

"Hey Kel, it's Jamie, can you send a unit or two over to the jail? I hate to call 9-1-1 but I want to make sure it's recorded. We've got some trouble-makers starting up again and I want it documented that we called again."

"You've got it, pal, they're on the way as we speak. Non-emergency?"

"Oh yeah, just ASAP if you know what I mean."

"Done!"

"Okay, I'll call ya later when it slows down to talk about some serious fishing."

"Deal, pardner."

I hang up and the city officers are already at the sally port, also known as the booking garage door. They are being buzzed in. They will probably go in and help the guards split up the prisoners. This is not normally something they call the officers in off the road for, but they have some pretty high-profile and gnarly bad guys this time, so it makes sense.

Jamie and I have fished together for a few years now. Mostly we start off at a dock or a pier or we will jump aboard with anyone else willing to take a couple of "girls" out on their fishing excursion. This year Jamie surprised everyone and bought her own bass boat. Not bad for a girl who cuts her worms with a fillet knife so she doesn't have to feel them being pulled apart. She is also pretty amazing as a corrections officer. Once I did a photography project for a college photojournalism class with black and white photography. Jamie opened and closed cell doors for areas where I had never been before. It was scary and some parts of it were so putrid that I couldn't stomach being inside the cell. It seemed so void and at the same time very chilling. In my mind I revisit my decision about moving on or bumping back into the jail to be a guard. I am satisfied with my decision. I ask Jamie how she can put up with it all. She goes into depth about how most of the guys in jail have just made unwise choices. They aren't genuinely bad. She has a soft spot for most of them. Sometimes I think she treats the inmates as if she is their little sister or something, the way she speaks to them. I will catch her telling them to hang on a sec and she will be sure they get their razor for a shave. She is courteous, polite, and always professional. The fishing side of her is my favorite part. We can pull some mean bass out of the bayous. At first, we waste a lot of time motoring back and forth to shore for potty breaks because we would laugh so hard. Eventually we learned to stop drinking coffee a couple of hours before we launch. Then we fish our hearts out. While we fish, we nary discuss work, the calls, the prisoners, or the bleakness of our jobs. We are content to just be two girls on a boat in a bayou, fishing.

Things start to flow fairly well in our 9-1-1 center, especially after figuring out the phones, the computers, the policies of which agencies took calls of people who were locked out of their cars and whatever else there was pertinent to their local ordinances. We rely on each other a lot and in turn have to train a few new people who come in knowing nothing at all. We take a lot of pride in our center. We clean, we decorate, and we keep it tidy. For a center with the growing pains that we are about to go through, it is the best center around. We know we have it made. We would complain about the equipment. That's what we do. We need to have all of the most convenient, efficient, and effective tools available. And they've got to work one hundred percent of the time. We want everything to work perfectly so when that officer, firefighter, or paramedic needs us, we can give them all of the pertinent and absolute information we have. We must be comfortable, alert, and focused for the next emergency call that comes in. The chairs we sit in are not always comfortable. And heaven forbid you find one that fits your…ah-hem…physique, then someone else claims it for the shift before you do. Arrghh!

We know how to take the call, dispatch the call, and give the people what they need. And they are all learning how to use those three simple numbers quite well!

"9-1-1."

"Yeah, I was just robbed."

"What do you mean by 'robbed'?"

"I was at the bar, and when I just came home, I found my door kicked open and my television and VCR and stereo are gone."

"What's your address?"

"Shit—you should have that on your screen. You need to get someone here right now."

"I understand, sir, but I must verify that the address is correct."

After more explanations, he gives me the numbers and the street, and I verify the city and send the correct officers. All the while, I try to make sure my caller is safe.

"Sir, are you the only one in the home? Is there any way you can go next door and call me from there in case there is someone still in the house?"

"Shit no, I'm sure it was my bitch girlfriend. She probably got pissed at me being at the bar again and had her new friend help her take all my shit. Well, this shit ain't cool."

"Okay, so you seem to be saying that you are safe to remain there until the police arrive?"

"Oh yeah. Hell, where are they? Are they here yet? I gotta take a piss."

"Okay sir, if you feel that there is no one else in the house, you can do that, and I'll advise my responding officers."

With technology advancing quicker than we know what we will use it for, this seems the perfect opportunity to use the mobile data computer terminal in the police units. I look up to see who is dispatched by the city dispatcher and send a message to that police officer.

"Be advised, the homeowner is there. He might be in the bathroom when you get there. He's been at the bar and couldn't hold it any longer. Krr."

(From MDT car C32.) "So no shoot he who walks out of BR."

That's short for him understanding not to shoot the guy coming out of the bathroom. Clearly the memo that says you

52

aren't supposed to type and drive is sometimes overlooked. The laptops are the best things since sliced bread. The officers type us, we type them, and we save a lot of air time. It clarifies calls, passes the time, and basically is another avenue for getting the job done. The other end of that is it can become a problem when they forget to treat it like any other radio frequency that is recorded. For the most part, it is an invaluable tool. Like the time Sgt. Davids was logged on and responding to headquarters for duty. Since he wasn't exactly a patrol unit, we pretty much leave those guys alone, until early one morning when someone called in saying a cruiser was just t-boned (struck in the side) at an intersection. We didn't have to look any further than our maps to see that his computer-provided AVL (automatic vehicle locator) showed his car stopped at an intersection. After a quick roll call of units, we knew it was him. He was seriously injured and we all held our breaths until they could cut him out of his patrol car. The calls that came in describing the scene were horrendous. As dispatchers do, we all imagined the worst. It took a great deal of time to get an ambulance to him because of the fog. Then it was not possible to use the air ambulance because of the fog. It became eerily quiet while all of the officers did their job without much chatter because they all were thinking, "What if it was me?" We thought the same thing about every one of them, so we worried a hundred times more. (Like good dispatchers we upped the ante wherever we could.) It turned out he was badly bruised and plenty broken up on the inside. He was going to make it and with plenty of therapy over the next twelve months, he did make it back. He walked at first with a cane and eventually he came full circle. I hugged him recently. He made it to retirement. One more call answered!

With this new technology we see who is calling us before we pick up the phone. The ANI (automatic number identification) and ALI (automatic location identification) are a vast improvement. We can actually see that the pay phone at the corner store is ringing repeatedly from kids calling in prank calls. We send a patrol car and stall for time.

We hear on the radio, "Charlie 21 central." Officer Lucas is panting like he is running. The city police dispatcher answers right away.

"Go ahead, Charlie."

"Two juvies in custody, en route to the station for interviews and phone calls to parents."

"Ten-four, Charlie, and thank you very much!"

"To serve and protect, ma'am," he answers with a smile in his voice.

I'm sure he isn't so much pleased that he caused them to stop harassing us as much as he is glad he caught them and had a nice time rounding them up. Either way, it is a nice ending to this shift. I pack up to head home around 2200 hours (10:00 pm).

I like the job very much still. I greatly enjoy helping people. I like the cops; they truly are the good guys. The uniforms make them seem different, but we see past the brown or blue and take them as they are. They put their lives on the line every day and they tell us things like, "I could never do this job. I could never sit here and take the crap on the phone like you guys do. I'd have to drive to their house and arrest their dumb-asses."

We take it as its own weird compliment and reciprocate.

"Well, there are pluses; after all, we get to go home when the shift ends. We don't have to submit reports, stand in the weather, and have people take punches at us or piss on our shoes." We laugh at each other's view of both sides of the radio. Underneath it all, as dispatchers we all know it is our primary job to make sure that everyone who starts their shift with us goes home the same way they come in; in one piece and alive and well.

Then it happens. It is December 13, 1994. I have just gotten into a big bathtub full of bubbles when I hear the yell from the other room.

"You'd better come look at this. The television station has a news crawler on the bottom of the TV saying an officer was shot in the city of Grand Harbor." They interrupt prime time local programming to report on the officer down. They say they do not know who yet or the extent of injuries.

I dress lightning fast and grab my car keys.

"Are you going in?"

"I have to. I don't know who it was and I have to be there for them."

I stand frozen and watch the broadcaster say over and over that they don't know which officer or the condition of that officer, but it appears that it was the result of a jail break. My heart sinks. I know a lot of people in the jail and on the road. My mind is swirling as to who might be involved. I call into work quickly before I run out the door.

"9-1-1."

"It's me, Kelly, what do you need?"

"Just come in."

"I'm on the way."

That's all I have to hear. I fly out the door and the entire seven-mile drive seems to be a flicker in time. I arrive to find people crying and in shock. The dispatch center has been filled with replacements for the dispatchers who were on duty for the "incident." I sit down at police radio. I start putting together all of the snippets of information. I hear bits and pieces and share bits and pieces. I take phone calls from police officers from everywhere asking who.

"It's Scott. Scott Flannery. The kid from Grand Harbor who was still pretty new. Good guy. Really good guy."

"Is he dead? The news isn't saying yet," Officer Brian asks.

"There was a bit of a standoff after the guy shot Scott. The state police ordered him to drop his weapon and they took him into custody. Yeah, I'm sorry, Brian, he's gone. I understand they tried to get to him in time, but he basically died there at the scene."

Silence and then sobs. Then a quick "Who got hurt at the jail?"

"Two guards. They took them by surprise and beat them up pretty bad. Callie is at the hospital, and Joe is going to be okay, physically."

He regains his composure for a second. "Thanks, Kel, you okay?"

"Yeah, thanks." We both hang up.

I feel so numb. I look over at Hank who is manning fire dispatch. He looks at me and asks if I need anything.

"Nope, but I'm glad you're here, bud."

"Yeah, same to ya."

He has raced in to get here and help out as well. Now we both sit and try to put the pieces together. Only we don't know what the pieces are or where they are supposed to fit. After a couple of hours of tips and sightings of the second bad guy who is still outstanding, we hear that the neighboring county has picked him up. I announce it over the air and the radio clicks seem to never stop.

Now what? The command post has been disbanded. Everyone has stopped searching. Now we all hold our breaths hoping that the guards are okay. I wonder…

What if I had been sitting the chair? Could I have stopped the officer from approaching that vehicle on the traffic stop? Would I have said something different to him that made him pause and wait a second for the back-up unit to get there? Would it have made a difference? Would he have listened to anyone? He was told that his additional unit was right behind him. Why would he approach that car? I know after the fact that he never had a clue the bad guy was lying down in the back seat with the 30-06 shotgun alongside him. We found out afterwards that the gun was fired as soon as the bad guy saw Scott's uniform. We heard later that the wound entry was Scott's femoral artery and he bled out immediately in front of the flower shop in the middle of the boulevard. We will never know what he was thinking. We will never know if we could have made a difference, but we know we've got to keep the rest of them safe, right now, at this moment.

Hank gets up and goes to get us some coffee. The phones are

eerily silent. The updates on the television stations must be letting people know the circumstances, so they aren't bothering to call us anymore tonight. The petty loud music complaints and such just aren't worth it in the grand scheme of things, I guess.

The door buzzes and Hank and I jump. It's a couple of state troopers. There is nothing for them to do at this hour, so they have stopped to check on us. They bring us burgers from the local fast food place before it closed up for the night. They knew we came in at a moment's notice and didn't know if we needed food. Hank begins to chow down.

Then the most amazing thing happens. The troopers stand on either side of our consoles. They aren't really at attention, but almost. They are silent. I've been to too many officer funerals and the honor guard scene is the most wrenching. Those guys guard the casket with full honor and pride, and here they are in a way, guarding us. They never utter a word. They watch us. They anticipate our every need, so when I lift my coffee cup and find the coffee must have evaporated, the trooper is there with the coffee pot before I can stand. It is awesome and weird and surreal all at once. To this day, I don't know if we ever thanked them. Or maybe it was their way of thanking us for always taking care of them. Either way, it was the most touching thing I have ever experienced.

Fear is an unexplained phenomenon. People can let it rule their lives, or meet it head on with guts and grit. Scott did that. He knew there were scary people out there. We all know there are lots of bad people out there. Dispatch hears more than we ever pass on. We try to get the responders from point A to point B safely and timely and well-prepared. We don't give the responders all the crap that is handed to us. We sort the call out in its entirety and give them the basics. Sure, we tell them if there is any reason to worry or to keep their eyes open extra. Unfortunately, we cannot look into a crystal ball and see that one bad guy about to take a shot at a good guy. Like our friends in uniforms teach us, we meet the situation head on. Each shift, we try to make a difference. We use our words, our voice, our tone, and our familiarity with them to make them listen to us. We rule out fear so they can be safe. So we don't have to wonder "what if?"

Companionship

It is weird when Jamie finally calls me the next morning. I ask her how she is doing before she can ask me. She tells me that she has been up to the hospital to see Callie. I ask her how things are going.

"She's holding her own. She's a tough cookie."

"Yeah, I hope so."

"Kel, ya know…"

"Yeah, Jamie, I know. I know damn well it could have been you. I know after their last try that you've still got bruises and pains from those bastards."

"Well, that wasn't exactly what I was going to say. I was going to ask where we are going fishing this spring, since my boat won't fit in at the usual dock."

I am about to cry and she can tell. She made me laugh like usual. Here we are talking about life and death and the fact that it could have been her, it could have been worse, it coulda, woulda, shoulda again. And she's talking about fishing. Ya gotta love having weird friends.

"Hang on, buddy, I gotta getta phone," I tell Jamie.

"9-1-1."

"I just want to tell you people that I am thinking of you. This is the Christmas season and you folks do things for us that we just take for granted. So I just wanted to quickly call and thank you."

"Well thank you, sir, and I will be sure to pass it along to all of our public safety community."

"Okay, thank you."

"Jamie?"

"Yeah, that was quick."

"Yeah, lots of folks calling in constantly to thank us. It's weird. Sometimes I want to smack them upside the head and say 'are you nuts? This is the freakin' 9-1-1 line.' I think that's the only thing that makes me focus and get them off the phone before I start cryin'."

"Well, you do a great job. I'm so glad that you reported to duty that night and helped everyone out. I heard Tom say that once he heard your voice, he knew that everything was going to be okay. It's like they were all driving around in this daze and didn't have a clue what to do."

"Yeah, it felt like that in here, too. Hank and I just sat here drinking coffee all night."

"Wow—you guys have it made." There's a futile attempt at a laugh, then, "Uh, er, uh, sorry 'bout that."

"It's okay, I know what you meant. I know you're trying to be funny and all. I just can't laugh yet. I want to blame someone and I don't know who."

"Well, we could blame the bad guy, but I don't know what good it will do us."

Always the beacon of hope and fun, my buddy is okay, and she and I will face this crap alongside everyone else.

"You sitting with dispatch at the funeral?"

"Yeah, I hope they remember to include us."

"I'll make sure to tell them. I'll be with all the corrections folks. And Callie says she's going to be there no matter what. So I might be sticking close to her."

"Okay, buddy. It ought to be some event, huh?"

"Yeah! It'll be good for us."

"Okay, I'll talk more with you later tonight, I gotta get another phone."

"Okay, bye."

"9-1-1."

"Yes, can you tell me the time and date of Scott's funeral? I want to bring my kids so they can say good-bye to a hero."

That about does me in. I cannot answer another line.

"Betty, that's it, I'm going to have a smoke."

"Okay, I think I'll join ya."

She assigns someone else to take my dispatch radio, and as my supervisor now, she walks me outside. Nowadays, this might be considered coaching or some kind of debriefing. Back then, it was called "smoke'm if you got'em."

We talk a bit. And it helps somewhat. We never know what we are supposed to do or say to people, especially to each other. Folks would call and tell us that if we needed anything to just call. Heck, how am I supposed to know what I need or my colleagues need, or the officers need at this time? I think for now we just need time. Betty and I smoke, talk about some small talk, and try to make light of some things. We really don't know what to say to each other. I think she just senses that I needed someone to stand by me. In the coming days, some of the female officers stop by the dispatch center and ask me to braid their hair for the funeral. It is the least I can do.

The day of the funeral comes. It is so overwhelming that my knees buckle. I did not imagine all these shades of blue uniforms adorned with badges covered with a black band across the middle. There are literally hundreds of police cars and fire trucks and ambulances. As dispatchers standing beside the men and women we protect, we march in formation, we file in formation, we salute in formation, we cry in formation. I pass by his casket so slowly that I think I am walking through a haze. I hurry to catch up and imagine that they must have run out of seats in the church. Sure enough, we are escorted up to the front, left side for the remaining chairs. Then there are more officers filing in. They come from all over the United States and Canada. They line the walls, the walkways, and all of the open spaces in the church. They fill it up and stand at attention throughout the entire service. Some cry, some look stoic, some wink at ya if you catch their eye. They all know it could be them up there. We all know it. And we all live our lives in defiance of it. We bury Scott on a cold December day. We say good-bye to a hero collectively. There is the honor guard, the twenty-one gun salute, the bagpipes, and the sign off of his unit number on the air. There isn't a dry eye anywhere. As dispatchers, we tell these guys daily; it's my job to make sure you go home the same way you come in to this shift. We send Scott on with honor and prestige because we care enough to send the very best. In the funeral procession, riding in the back of a police cruiser with fellow officers, I see the citizens lining the streets this cold and snowy day. A child stands next to his father and salutes as the police cars go by. I sob so hard my chest feels like it will cave in.

In an instant, it is done and he is gone and everyone reports to duty to continue answering calls. It is hard to imagine moving on and I try to make sense of it as we are all in some sort of trance or shock. We live day to day on extra alert and dig a little deeper to find information on bad guys so we can avoid any more tragedies.

Dispatching cops became a test of wills a few days after the funeral. Some officers felt consciously or subconsciously that they needed to test the system or the gods or whatever. The stops were haphazard or not called out at all. They took more risks. They dismissed the idea of anything to do with safety. They tempted the gods to defy them. They were on a mission, they wanted vengeance, and we were caught in the middle. There was no special training, no debriefing, and no intervention to help guide us. We rambled on. In the dispatch center, we felt left behind. We were hurting and felt forgotten. We moved on the best we knew how. We stomped our feet and demanded that the road officers straighten up. They eventually did. They needed to work out their own issues and we had to let them. We just wanted them to know that we weren't the bad guys. Not all of them were experiencing troubles. Some reported to duty, did the job as always, and went home smiling. As the officers moved on, we did our best to help them. One of the officers who worked for a smaller police department for a number of years could always be counted on to bring us out of our funk. We all loved him because English was his second language. And we knew we were in for some excitement when he was going to a hot call or in a pursuit.

"Charlie 12 central."

"Charlie 12, go ahead."

"Washington y Elm con el auto." He would give out suspect and vehicle descriptions in Spanish. We were lucky enough that other officers on the department could translate for us. It was muy rápido and he usually caught us by surprise! No matter what, we were always there for our first responders. We knew we had to be their lifeline. Likewise, we knew that our profession was evolving and becoming more technological, more advanced, more important. We collectively recognized that we were growing up as a profession.

For me to grow up and on to my goal of becoming a director someday, I knew I needed to advance up the ranks within the center. Whether it was timing, or fate, or luck, I like to think of it as raw determination mixed with a healthy dose of maturity, thanks to life experiences. Either way, the day came when I was finally promoted to shift supervisor. I was finally there. I found my spot alongside the folks I had admired for so many years. Sheila, Betty, and Joe had inspired, motivated, and believed in me. And here I was, about to lead my own shift of dispatchers. I realized quickly how much I didn't know, instead of how much I thought I knew. Also, I learned quickly the difference between being a dispatcher and letting others dispatch. I tried to follow the lead of my other supervisors, but they were nowhere to be found. Literally, I got to see them for a few minutes before and after the shift to ask what to do. I was sent off to one class of leadership training that taught me that my new position was something akin to being a monkey in the middle; at least that's how the trainer described it. I felt like a foreigner in a new land as this position had very little to do with dispatch.

The dispatchers knew what they were doing. And I knew what they were capable of when I was their peer. What changed? Finally one of my most loving dispatchers said to me one shift,

"Kelly, shut the eff up and trust us to do our jobs." Enough said. I got sent to a management school shortly after that. It was for two days. It was interesting. It went something like this.

This instructor stood up front and said, "You have worked your tail off for years and you have finally come into a little more money, lots more opportunities to make decisions, tons of sarcasm from those you once worked alongside, and having to be in the middle between the boss and the folks doing the grunt work. Well, congratulations, you are now middle management, and folks, middle management sucks." That was the gist of the training. I thought, "What about the respect, the responsibility, and the rewards?" I didn't know I had to invent those.

I sometimes felt like an air traffic controller. Oftentimes, I stood on my toes (from excitement) and directed my folks from behind my console. When it was busy, it was awe-inspiring. They were all so good at what they did that my challenge was to keep up with them and at the same time move beyond them and think like an administrator. Good dispatchers grow really good supervisors. (The same case could be made here for the other end of the spectrum.) I tried to make sense out of what the higher-ups would want and how to make it happen. My shift loved me for it. They respected that I let them do their job and coached them when they needed it. They let me guide them and grow them since I always reminded them that someday, they could be the one running the place. They would laugh.

I will never forget supervising and coaching Sally. She was struggling with her attitude and depression and health and family issues. She felt herself doubting the callers more and more. The neat thing is that together, we worked at discovering what had changed to make her so disgruntled with her job. She came to the conclusion on her own, of course. I merely helped point the way. The callers were the same as the day she took her first call. Sally needed to focus and she realized she wasn't doing that for the callers. She and I worked on it together. Then one day I listened in as she took a medical call. I picked up the line after I saw Sally reach for her medical dispatch cards. The first part of the conversation was played back later for all of us to learn from.

"9-1-1."

"Yes, I am sure that my husband has passed in his sleep, in his chair. Can you send someone, dear?"

This little female voice was plain and simple and she was so matter of fact that I understood the look of puzzlement on Sally's face. Sally grabbed for her medical cards to give instructions.

"Are you sure he is dead?"

"Oh yes, dear, he's passed."

"Okay, can you pull him out of his chair onto the floor to give him CPR?"

"No, you don't understand, dear, he's passed, and he's too heavy for me to do that. I just want to be with him now."

Sally looked over at me, covered her headset microphone tube with her finger, and asked what she should do.

I shrugged my shoulders and said, "Just be with her. It's okay."

We were trained so hard to do everything by the medical dispatch cards. There weren't any cards that said what to do if a little old lady calls you to tell that her husband had passed and how to give her assistance. Sally placed the cards back on the top of her console for the next medical call since she didn't need them for this one.

"Okay, ma'am, I'm here with you and I'm sending the ambulance."

"Please ask them not to use their sirens."

"Okay, Mrs. Johnson, I will tell them."

I heard Sally advise the ambulance and then I kept a visual on her while I hung up to answer another call. I looked over at Sally and I saw her listening and wiping her eyes. Later we discussed the call.

"Kel, it was the reason I'm here. I have worked my whole life to handle that call. That little old lady shared her last moments with her husband with me. She just talked to him."

"What do you mean she talked to him?"

"She told him how much she loved him. She thanked him for their sixty years together and she told him how much she enjoyed his sense of humor." She paused to catch her breath.

"Wow, Sally, that must have been hard to listen to."

"Yes and no, it was so cool. It was the most amazing thing I have ever been a part of. I am so honored she would share that time with me. I don't know if she meant to, but it was so awesome."

I was proud of Sally. By the same token, I was grateful that she was a part of it. It gave her what she needed. I could sense that she was filled with a renewed spirit. A dispatcher rarely gets the closure from the call they played such an active role in. We never know if we really helped or how much we have helped or what we might have done differently to help. We listen intently and do the best we can according to procedure and according to the golden rule. In the days that followed, Sally told everyone about her call. Each time she recounted the details of the recliner, and the little old lady's words, she was lifted to a higher place. I could see that she was touched deep inside by this act. I was never as proud of anyone as I was that day to see Sally move from such a dark place to a place of honor and integrity. She is one of the very best in the business. In my heart, she always will be the beautiful soul who comforted a woman when no one else was there. Sally was a companion to a woman who lost her soul mate. I had found a way to motivate my staff for years to come by always being there for them, and asking them, "What changed?"

Keeping in mind the humanity of the job and considering how we are always human, we sometimes make human mistakes, of course. Sometimes our brains aren't quite engaged when we open our mouth and key that microphone. We all do it, some more often than others. My buddy, Sally, did it once, in giving out a license plate.

"Car 31 copy your plate info."

"Go ahead, central."

"Plate is negative on a Mercury Benz." She perfectly stated that the plate was not stolen and yet it should accurately be displayed on a vehicle type that Sally just made up.

She never paused, and never thought twice about the abbreviation of "Merc" possibly being a Mercedes. I reciprocated shortly after that in trying to dispatch a medical for an officer to respond and assist the ambulance.

"Car 731, copy a medical."

"Go ahead."

"Assist the ambulance at 21 North Street on an abdimal, abdimal, abdimal…uh, stomach pains."

I couldn't lift my foot off the foot pedal and for some reason, my mouth couldn't formulate the word "abdominal." Everyone got a good laugh at that one, especially Sally.

There are so many of those quirks, conundrums, or freaky happenings that sometimes I think the public must listen to us solely for entertainment.

Being a supervisor was never anything like I thought it would be. I thought I could still dispatch as well as speak for, and on behalf of, my dispatchers. I thought I could make things right by being straightforward with the bosses. I figured I could make things better, period. Try as I might, it often seemed I couldn't ever make things right. I would fix one thing and they would bring me another. I tired the bosses and they weren't as receptive after the first dozen approaches. They often sent me back to the masses saying something like, "Bring a solution instead of problems." I just didn't know what that looked like in order to model it. What I could do was be a mediator between my officers and my dispatchers. I knew the officers' job wasn't easy and I knew that my dispatchers were only trying to take care of them as I (and others) had taught them over the years. As a supervisor, I wasn't on the air much anymore. The dispatchers allowed me to help out when I made them take breaks. Being dispatchers, they all can be control freaks and not want to miss anything by being away too long. I had to beg, threaten, and beat them into taking a genuine break from the console. As I settled into the background, I became content to change my focus. The dispatchers became more comfortable with me interpreting their behaviors and body language.

For example, one of my female dispatchers was clearly not a morning person. After several mornings of being cheery and welcoming with her, I realized that she needed to settle in and have her Coke and wake up her own way in order to be considered sociable by about nine a.m. Then I would approach her and see how things were going. She eventually noticed that I was doing this and questioned me on it. I explained that I was not trying to make her mornings miserable; rather, I was just happy to have rotated to day shifts and was glad when she walked in the door. She said she never saw it from my angle and from then on when she came in for her day shift, she said "good morning" first. It wasn't all cheery and smiley; rather, it was matter of fact. And it was okay too! I gratefully exclaimed back to her without much ado that it was indeed a good morning now that she was here!

Dispatchers are a different breed of people. Who knows why we do the job? There certainly isn't much appreciation or attention. Some of us like the lack of attention; some of us would like to be acknowledged once in a while. Over and over you read the "thank yous" in the local paper from people who thank the police or firefighters or paramedics for responding so quickly. Most never wonder how they did that. How did they get going so quickly and know what to expect and be routed to the exact location? Dispatching is a thankless job. We just have to know that we make a difference and we have to remind each other.

One amazing stormy spring weekend, my staff of three dispatchers had worked some pretty incredible storms for most of their assigned weekend shifts. By the end of their rotation early Sunday morning, I could tell they were beat. I let them read, do crosswords, play solitaire, and wait for the next emergencies to come along. We didn't interact much and didn't have a lot to say. I answered the phones first and let them have a breather. Even the deputies were surprised to hear me, which I took advantage of to tell them how busy and organized and professional my staff was on that weekend! As I looked over at the radar screen for the weather, I noticed a line of thunderstorms hitting the shoreline. It was a very long line of storms, and curiously as it touched land at the north end, the color changed to blood red. It wasn't green for rain, or pink for rain-snow; rather, it was very dark, crimson red. Then the reports started to come across the wire. There were very strong winds, trees down, roofs being ripped off, and small buildings being toppled. It did not look good. I knew my dispatchers were tired of storms. This one was scheduled to hit an hour or two before the end of their shift. I had to clue them in.

"Would you come take a look at this?"

One by one they came over to the radar screen and agreed that we needed to be ready. At least there was some advance warning with this storm. The previous storms just sprouted up and pounded us all day and night. We started to prepare. We got out our forms for the utilities and for the power companies. We faxed reports of trees down on power lines or hot power lines down, or power outages and such. It helped us to keep track of where the problems could be pinpointed in the county as well.

As we got out our boxes of paperwork assigned to each console, somebody joked, "Watch, it'll dud on us now that we're getting prepared."

"Well, I hope so. We will be ready if it doesn't," I reassured them and sent a page out to ask for more help. Just in case.

Five o'clock on the nose it hit us like a freight train. There were no weather service notices, no warnings. It was five in the morning on a Sunday and nobody was awake or aware of what was coming on shore to brutally assault our community. The phones started ringing and they never stopped for well over three hours.

"9-1-1."

"Yes, a tree fell on my house."

"What is your address?" Address given and verified.

"Is there anyone injured or any smoke or fire?"

"No, but I don't know what I am going to do with this tree!"

"Okay, thank you for calling." Disconnect.

"9-1-1."

"There's a tree down on my garage and my car is stuck inside."

"Anyone injured?"

"Well, no."

"Any smoke or fire?"

"No."

"Okay." Disconnect.

There was no time in between calls to add any extra words. The questions became painfully obvious that we were investigating any injury or fire. We could not pick up the lines fast enough. As soon as we answered one call, there were visibly six more in the queue waiting to be answered. There were dozens and dozens more not getting through to us. We got the calls and teletypes from other centers taking our calls. There were trees down, lines down, too many to keep track of. Then, without notice, our computers were frozen. The new incident entry screens they had taught us to use instead of writing things on paper went down for the Sunday morning back-up. We were stuck. I heard everyone trying to dig up paper and pens.

Then I heard them in the background asking caller after caller, "Any smoke, fire, or injuries? Okay, thank you." Disconnect.

Verbiage is quick, concise, tight, and emotionless. We might sound like we are in a hurry. We are. The calls are from the north end of the county. They appear to be only the north quarter of the county, as a matter of fact. I take a quick look at the radar. Sure enough, there are no calls to the south because it hasn't struck there yet. The line of storms is tilted to the northeast on the top of the line. The bottom, which is still a ways out, is lingering from the southwest. That should buy us some time. This observation took all of about four seconds and I still couldn't communicate

70

it to my team. I overheard a voice on the fire south radio channel trying to hail us. I answer up.

"This is central, go ahead unit calling."

"I've been trying to reach you on fire north, but I can't. And I can't get through on the phone. We are here at the state park and we have campers blown across the entire park. We have campers that have rolled over, tents that have blown away, and campers rolled onto cars."

"I'm clear on your traffic. Are you reporting any injuries or need for Fire/EMS?"

"Uh, I guess not. But it's a heck of a mess down here."

"I'm clear. If you need ambulance or fire, let me know ASAP on this channel, clear?"

"Clear central, I'll check."

I go back to answering phones. Surely there have to be injuries. He just hasn't found them yet. I am sure this wicked storm is as dangerous as it is ferocious. Phone call after phone call, we continue to answer.

"9-1-1."

"We are camping at the state park."

"Are you injured?"

"No, but there's a camper on top of us."

"What do you mean on top of you?"

"We heard the storm come in and left our tent to ride it out in our car. This big ass motor home camper in the next site flipped upside down on top of our car. The roof is dented in."

"Are you all okay?"

"Yeah, but we might need some help getting out of here."

"How about the folks in the motor home?"

"Oh, they're fine. The old guy just crawled out the front windshield and helped his wife out too. They asked if we are okay and we told them to get some help but that we are fine for now."

"Wow." I nearly exhale.

"Yeah, wow, it's some crazy storm."

"Okay, if everyone is okay, I'll let the folks responding that way know about you. What kind of car?"

He laughs at the question. "The one with the camper on top of it."

I hang up and hear my staff still trying to keep up with the phone calls. It has been forty-five minutes of nonstop calls. This is ridiculous. I need help in here. Where is the answer to the page I put out forty-five minutes ago? I grab another phone after taking another quick look at the radar. The storm has softened. The south end looks like it will only see rain, if that.

"9-1-1, are you reporting injuries or fire?"

"Well, yes, my husband is having chest pains."

"Okay, what is your address?"

I get all of the details and catch my breath myself while I do a pre-alert on the fire-medical radio channel. The department I have to tone for the medical has not seen any action yet because we haven't had anything dangerous or threatening in their area. The only ones who might be listening are the ones waiting for the storm to dip into their area. In the meantime, this isn't storm related exactly, and I needed to get them rolling in spite of all of the other storm activity.

I start off by saying, "Grand Harbor Township Fire Rescue, stand by for (a call of) Chest Pains and they're not mine!" I set off the tones. I glance quickly around the room and I notice all three of my dispatchers rise out of their seats as they look over at me. They look at each other as if we are all frozen in time.

"Did she just say that on the air?"

"Yeah, I heard her."

I smile at them all after the tones finish and I repeat the announcement of a chest pains medical and announce the address of the caller. They all slowly sit back down and smile while they continue to answer the endless stream of phone calls.

It was all I could do. I needed to break the pace and let them know we were doing everything that we were capable of. They are doing a great job and I didn't know how to tell them. The worst thing a dispatcher can ever feel is out of control. That morning we all not only felt out of control, but we tried to survive it. We could not control or fix anything. We could only maintain and stay the course. We helped where we could and we felt totally out of our element. Our next shift together, we "debriefed" each other.

"Did you guys drive around and see the effects of the storm?" I ask them.

"Yeah, I took a trip out north shore and it was a mess." Jamie shakes his head.

"Heck, I had to change directions three times to get home." Don is laughing.

"Well, I went to the state park and it was total chaos like they said," I tell them.

As dispatchers, we paint the canvas with eccentric pictures from our mind's eye. We don't see the real thing. We only imagine. Since this storm had been touted as the storm of the century for this area, it was noteworthy on many fronts. It was good to come together and talk about it. We needed to express what we were feeling that night.

"I just felt so helpless," says Maggie.

"I heard Kelly over there say stand by for chest pains and they weren't hers and I about lost it. Or I thought she had lost it," says Don.

"Nah, I didn't lose it, none of us lost it. We just needed to be reminded that we were all still here in the middle of it," I tell them.

"Well, it brought me back to reality," chimes in Jamie.

"I'm glad to hear that. I was hoping to let you guys know somehow that it was understandable that we were doing everything we could," I assure them.

"Yeah, but what a freakin' stupid time for the computers to go down," Don reminds me.

"Oh that. I got a note from the boss after my summary that they changed it."

"Changed what?"

"They made it so the computer asks if it's okay to do a back-up and the supervisor has to answer yes or no," I explain.

"Well, that's good." Maggie smiles.

"Good and not so good maybe. It does give us an option. In the future, if I don't notice the radar and go ahead and click yes, we will still have to go through what we did," I remind them.

"Oh yeah."

"This is why I want you to see how much you did right."

We re-hash the whole storm from beginning to end. I take some more ribbing about having chest pains and to this day, I never regret saying what I did on the air. We needed the break from the pandemonium. People were scared. They were afraid for their lives, and all we could ask was if there were injuries or fire. We felt absolutely helpless. We talked about what to do next time and one of the things we agreed upon was to add a playful form to the box addressing the concern of "What to do if you think you're having chest pains in the midst of the storm."

Being a supervisor is not always easy. It's not fun when it comes to critiquing or counseling the folks who do such a thankless job. It feels like adding fuel to the fire. Then there's the burned-out employee. How do you counsel someone who is only biding time? How do you re-instill the courage and honor of doing this job again? How do you help them see themselves as you and everyone else sees them? It is not pleasant. Everyone likes to vent. When one's venting interferes with another's growing and learning, then it's time to intervene.

For example, everyone had been complaining about Hank for some time. His profanity. His criticisms. His attitude. His belligerence. His belching, for gosh sake. No kidding, everyone was full of his loud and obnoxious belching. You know you feel too much like family when you have to tell someone to grow up and stop belching as if they are at home on their sofa watching a football game. Being a supervisor, and specifically, Hank's supervisor, I was tasked with taking him aside. Being younger than him, and female, I figured I had to appeal to him from some place he would identify. Thus began my coaching career of helping my dispatchers to actually improve.

"Hank, let's go smoke," I say during one shift.

"Why?" He's a sly ol' dog.

"I said so. And I see you're not really overworked there training the new guy, so I figure I can give you a few pointers."

Hank takes his feet down off the desk, slowly rolls his chair back, combs his hair like he's the Fonz from the Happy Days television show, and zips up his leather jacket as we head outside.

"Hank, let me start by saying that you know how much I admire you and your wit."

"Yeah?" He's suspicious but gracious.

"Yeah, so I need to ask your help. You know how folks see me as their peer still, and you know I'm trying hard to improve this place and be the best supervisor I can."

"Yeah, and from all that I hear, Kel, you're doing a great job. No—serious, I'm not blowing smoke up your ass or nothin'. Everyone's real glad you got the position. And I ain't heard anything negative at all. Everyone wants to make sure they work your rotation."

He's being serious. I can tell because he looks me in the eye and he is trying to talk to me like one of his kids. I've got his full attention!

"Well, then maybe you can help me out?"

"Sure, Kel, anything you want, name it."

"Look, I can't be everything to everyone. I need help. I'm trying to make it more professional in here, but I need your help. With the new kids and all, I can't be everywhere. So I really need you to look the part and, of course, follow my lead."

This is key with him because he respects good leadership. And he just told me that he approves of my leadership lately. So I take it a step further.

"I know you're out of here only too soon. And I'm going to miss you a ton when you're gone. I will have a hole in my heart because you'll be off fishing somewhere and I'll be left here to sit and think about you."

He looks at me and a smile breaks out as he lowers his head and starts to shake it slowly, side to side. He's got it and he knows I've got him.

"What? What are you thinking?"

"Ya got me, Kel, I know what you're askin'."

"And? Can I count on you? You know I need you to be more professional and while it may be a stretch with the old habits that we're all used to, I really need you to step up."

"Yeah, I get your drift. Enough said. I can help you out for a few more months, or until I'm off your rotation." He grins at me and asks if I want another smoke.

"Hank, shame on you. You're a bad influence. I'll have another with ya, and I'll expect the professionalism to continue when I move to nights and you're still influencing people on days."

"All right, but just for you."

We both end our second smoke as quickly as it starts as we are paged to return to the center. We race inside through the locked doors.

"What's up?" I ask as I hit the door first.

"Car versus train, looks bad."

"Okay, what do we need yet?" I fire questions in between clips of radio traffic and calls that are still being answered, as well as being made to various agencies. Of course there are the media calls coming in, too. Someone overheard the radio traffic on a scanner. That's always what they do.

"Central dispatch." I answer the non-emergency line.

"This is Paul from the press, is this Kelly?"

"Yes, Paul, thanks for calling, you've got what we have. I can't make up anything for you, buddy."

He verifies the location and asks me three different ways if there is anything else I can tell him. Once upon a time I asked a reporter why they did that. He explained that they are taught to do it that way because they know we have to tell them nothing at first, and even the second time we find a way to rephrase saying nothing. By the third time we think of other things in an attempt to get rid of them. Hmmph. This was the most powerful piece of information I could have ever had about the "other side." For so many years I thought they just did it to annoy us. Now I could tell my folks to tell them "no" twice and then put them on hold for me. Never be tempted to go the third round. I'll tell them "no" two more times and put an end to it. Of course, it wasn't always like that. I became known to them on a first-name basis and we connected with a glimpse of truth. Honestly, I could tell someone like Paul, "No Paul, I can't do this right now, I have to make some other calls." And just like that, he understood. Were there times I could offer a bit more? Sure! I could give them a piece of information like, "You don't want to wake someone up to go out to this one. It's not that big." They trusted that. They figured it out on their own that it wasn't going to be newsworthy, but they believed in my discretion. It's that way with the cops, fire dudes (as I lovingly refer to them), and paramedics. Why shouldn't it be that way with the media? I know they just have a job to do. And when I need them, I sure want to be able to depend on them. This call isn't going to be an easy one. I have just been informed it is one of our officer's kids involved in the train crash.

"Kel, we need victim advocates and cars 1, 2, and 3 notified." Don is asking for the volunteer group who responds to help with critical incidents and stress during a tough call, as well as the sheriff, undersheriff, and road lieutenant. I send out the pages, which results in more phone calls.

"Kel, this is Rick. I see from the page that it is a car-train. Who is it?" the sheriff asks.

"It's Don G.'s teenage son and a friend. They tried to beat the train."

"Darn. Who do you have out there?"

I fill him in with who is where and who the command sergeant is. We make sure to get help to Officer Don and we keep him and his family tightly surrounded. This is no time for grieving to get the best of anyone.

I look around the room at my staff and I see their faces. I hear them tell the people on the other end of the phone who it is. I can tell who they are talking with by how they phrase the responses. If it is someone close to the family it is much warmer than the curt response given to media. It just happens that way. It keeps emotions in check

I have to get them breaks. I have to get them out of the room for a quick breather. I need them to EXHALE. It hits close to home like this. Everyone in this room either has a child the same age, or close, or has a relative this age. We all feel it. It is senseless. In a moment, a young life is gone too soon.

"9-1-1."

"I'm sorry to call 9-1-1 but I have a neighbor who is playing his music so loud that I can hardly hear my television."

"Okay, ma'am, what is your address?" I begin to gather the necessary info to send a car to the neighbor's and ask them to call it a night. She has no idea that a beloved teenager of one of our officers died. And she shouldn't have to know. She should know that her call is important enough to call us, so it's important enough for me to send her some assistance. Is it a 9-1-1 call? No, but I don't want to take the time to have her redial on the non-emergency number. I want to be normal for a second and enter a complaint that requires an officer to drive to the location and handle the complaint. A true professional is friendly, courteous, and takes the time to try to understand. It is more than a job at this point.

Empathy

Empathy is defined by Merriam Webster as:

"the action of understanding, being aware of, being sensitive to, and vicariously experiencing the feelings, thoughts, and experience of another of either the past or present without having the feelings, thoughts, and experience fully communicated in an objectively explicit manner."

In today's world, I teach and train dispatchers and supervisors that when we tell someone something that is positive or praiseworthy, we must mean it. We practice with Secret Buddies, a game we learned from the Big Book of Leadership Games. We give one another three bits of positive praise. I ask them to stand and face one another and use the word "you," not "they." I don't want them to talk about each other; rather, to each other. In the real world of what we do sitting at that console, we seldom rise over the monitors to look at the other person when we want to tell them something. Further, we might send it in an email or in a CAD message or via another electronic device. We fail to see the importance of "looking someone in the eye." We practice empathy on the phones every day, every shift, on every incident. Still, we are critically unable to empathize with our fellow coworkers about what they might be going through or how we might be able to help them through it. We say we care about each other because we spend as many, if not more, hours with them as we do our own families. Yet, our listening skills and pure understanding of our partners can be magnificently lacking. We are so practiced with callers that we fail to realize we have an obligation to remain courteous and professional with our colleagues. We forget that we are not exactly family, and it's not Thanksgiving dinner where everyone is fair game and continuous criticism is the sport.

The job is infiltrated enough by negativity. Other than a complaint department somewhere, I don't know where employees have to dine on such depression and dread for a continuous eight, ten, or twelve hours of every shift they work. If only it was a little old lady calling them a "butthead" once in a while. We should all be so lucky.

Practicing empathy from a supervisor's standpoint with a fellow dispatcher can be draining, to say the least. My squad used to delight in telling me that it was so difficult remembering how each supervisor liked running his or her shift. I would respond with, "That's correct, and of course we have it down pat dealing with all of your personalities and quirks since you guys outnumber us." My point was, they put the onus on us to understand them, not the other way around. I told myself that someday I would help them see the other side. Communication is truly a two-way street. Sometimes we forget that each of us plays an important part. On one occasion, I answer the ringing 9-1-1 call only to hear a small voice on the other end that sounds strangely like one of my lieutenants from the road patrol. The communication goes like this.

"9-1-1."

"Help me." (Then dead air.)

"What?"

"Help me." (Again dead air.)

I cannot imagine what this means. I sort of recognize the caller's voice.

"Is this you, Mark?"

"Yeah, I, uh, got your page, what do you need?" (Normal voice.)

"What the heck are …" I stop short, pause, and look at the 9-1-1 screen. We've had problems with that particular address of a bad guy on numerous occasions. My mind is moving in fast forward with questions I want to ask the lieutenant. I want to know why he is out there, who he is with, where the bad guy is, and why the hell is he calling me on a 9-1-1 line and asking me to help him.

"I will help you, tell me what you need."

"I can't. Tell me what you need already." (This is going to be a puzzle if he's answering questions with my questions or statements.)

He's being cryptic and it's scaring the crap out of me. I hunker down in my chair and close off the sounds of the room. Being the supervisor, I can do this knowing my folks are handling everything else in their own professional, quirky way.

"Okay, I'm going to ask you some yes/no questions and you tell me what you've got, agreed?"

"Okay, go."

"Are you alone?"

"No, uh Sergeant Danson is here, he can't come to the phone."

Great, now I know I have a less than bright lieutenant and an even dumber sergeant putting their butts on the line and except for them calling me on the 9-1-1 line, I wouldn't have a freakin' clue where they were.

"Are you both okay?"

"Oh yeah, not a problem."

"Do you need backup?"

"Eventually."

"Okay, if I'm hearing you correctly, you and the sarge are in a bad way with a bad guy and you will need backup but at your discretion. Do I have this correct so far?"

"Yeah, that's it."

Freakin' butt-pucker factor twelve. I feel the room spin.

I only understand much later that I am about to experience the phenomenon known as tunnel vision. I do not know what I've got and I'm trying to figure out how to get him help. As a lieutenant, you would think he would know better than to get himself into this mess. Then again, I'm never going to work the road, and I cannot for the life of me imagine how they got into this. I've just got to get them out.

I send a message over the mobile computer to the officer from that area, car 51: "Your location?"

He types me back quickly so I see that he's not tied up on something.

"I'm in the county at your disposal, ma'am."

He's nice, because he knows I run the world and can have my dispatchers send him to a thousand and one barking dog complaints. I smile to myself.

"Okay, I need you to quietly and covertly head towards the following address and await further instructions from me."

I prepare to type up the address for the next message as I am still engaged in conversation with my favorite lieutenant.

"Is this Joe, the guy we have a warrant for animal abuse?" I ask.

"Yeah…and more."

Okay, that ticks me off. Running him in-house and through LEIN all I can find is the animal abuse warrant. Now my lieutenant is telling me he must have charges for other things that I am unaware of. Or maybe now he has racked up a whole new set of charges. Again, my mind is racing.

"Is it safe to stay on the phone with me?"

"Yeah, I think you should let Don know that the schedule has that opening to be filled yet."

He's really scaring me now. The last time I played twenty questions and had some lady give me her Thanksgiving stuffing recipe, her husband had a gun and was waving and pointing it at every family member in the house.

"Okay, I'm going to take that as a yes. I want you to tell me this—is it just you three?"

"Yes."

"I've got car 51 moving that way in a stealth mode. Would you like him to stage?"

"Yes."

"Is there adequate coverage for 51 to hide and come in on foot?"

"Yes."

"Are you and the sarge armed?"

"No."

"Is he?"

"Yes."

"With a gun?"

"Yes, on the table."

I pause. I am taken aback at the last comment. He takes advantage of the pause. The bad guy is up and pacing in the background. I can hear him becoming agitated and therefore loud.

"He's got a gun on the table pointed at us. He wouldn't let me bring in my service revolver. He's on something and we were having a nice talk until about ten minutes ago when he drew on us. He only let me make the call to answer a page that I happened to get."

"Okay, is that him screaming?"

"Yes, have 51 stay way out of sight and not to come in on foot until you hear from me."

"Okay, sir."

I type quickly to 51 to make sure that he doesn't enter the premises in any way. I hear a voice faintly across the room. It's almost as if I'm in a vast, deep tunnel. I cannot focus on where the voice came from. I look about the room and it's like everything is in slow motion. I hear dispatcher Hank yelling my name over and over. Lisa claps her hands at me from the console closest to mine. I am startled, and everything whooshes back at me all at once.

"Hank, I'm talking with 51 on his mobile computer, leave him alone, but tell him not to enter the premises until I give him the okay. Tell him it's extremely dangerous. Are you clear?"

If at any moment in my supervisory career I needed my dispatchers to just do and not ask, this was one of them. I went back down into my hole to keep my lieutenant on the other end of the lifeline.

"Mark?"

"Yeah,"

"We'll help you."

"I know."

"I have 51 close by, waiting for your command. And I'm having another car slide that way as soon as he clears; 51 is the closest."

"Okay, that sounds good."

"The situation sounds bad in the background. Are you sure we're going to be okay here?"

He takes advantage again of the mad man's ranting.

"Kel, have 51 park on the southeast corner behind the building. Danson and I will walk him outside. He does not want to see any uniform or marked unit. Are you clear?"

I get from him that this guy is psycho and the lieutenant and sergeant are already compromised, so sending in anything marked would put their lives in danger. 51 is typing me like crazy, asking me where to set up and what they have and isn't this the icky bad guy type of comments and questions.

I type quickly in bold letters back to car 51: "51 – SET UP ON THE SE CORNER BEHIND THE BUILDING. Do not enter on foot until I tell you. Not my dispatcher, not anyone else, ME. Are you clear? This could be bad stuff, so tell me you get it."

"I'm clear and waiting for orders, Kel. I'm parked and waiting."

I think I scared him. Which I hope I did.

The lieutenant continues, "Okay, I believe we are heading outside. Danson has the guy convinced to step out for a smoke. I will lay the phone down. Tell 51 not to approach until I put my right hand in the air."

"Right hand in the air, I'm listening."

The phone is gently laid on the table or countertop. I hear the sergeant joking with the bad guy. I hear the scrape of the gun across the table. I hear the chairs scoot back. I hear the footsteps as they grow faint. I type to 51 to listen to me on another channel. He calls me on that channel instantly.

"51 to dispatch."

I jump to tell everyone in the room it is for me.

"51, do not approach until the lieutenant puts his right arm in the air."

"51 clear dispatch, right arm in air."

"21 dispatch, I'm headed his way, he filled me in and I am clear on taking cover."

Crap. Now what?

My dispatcher in charge of police dispatch just threw an ugly glance my way. I hear him mumble under his breath, "It sure would be nice to know what the hell my guys are doing."

"Hang on, Hank, I'll fill you in shortly, just trust me on this one."

The last thing in the world that a dispatcher wants to do is trust someone else with their guys. But just this once, or at least I hope this once, I believe I've earned the trust. I hear a lot of silence. I stand in my spot. I look over at my police dispatcher. Our eyes lock. He knows I'm not bluffing here.

"51—dispatch."

"Go ahead, 51." I let Hank answer his police unit.

"One in custody, scene is secure."

I sit down and exhale. I know what my dispatchers must have been feeling. I do not know what the lieutenant and sergeant were feeling. All I know is that they called for help and I had to deliver.

"9-1-1."

It's the lieutenant, and he's all friendly and cheery. "Hey, Kel, it's me, I just wanted to say thanks and you did a nice job."

"Yeah, well, I just want to say that if you ever pull a stunt like that again, I'll personally drive to the scene myself and kick you square in the ass. I don't care if this is a taped line. You scared me to death. I mean it."

"Yeah." He laughs nervously. "I know. I was really glad to hear your voice when I called. I didn't know who I'd get. I know everyone in there would have saved our butts, but I was very relieved when you picked up."

"You are not going to sweet-talk me right now. I am so freakin' mad. I cannot believe you. What were you thinking? Where was your weapon? Why did you guys enter like that? How come you didn't check out there?"

I hit him up with the whole barrage. I feel like I have a sudden case of diarrhea of the mouth. He laughs nervously again.

"Let me tell you, I didn't plan on it and neither did Danson. We were coming to talk to the guy about this warrant for a skinned cat."

"What skinned cat?"

"Oh, it was the initial warrant. Kel, you don't want to know what this asshole did to the cats he brought home. The neighbors were missing their cats on a daily basis. Anyhow, we pull into the drive, and he steps out onto the porch and says that Danson can come in to talk with him. But not me. He says he doesn't like the way I look."

"Well, that's good judgment on his part, I'd say," I tease him now.

"Yeah, but I'm not letting Danson go in there alone. So I stay quiet while Danson tells him I gotta come too. He asks us if we're armed."

"But you guys are in uniform?"

"No, not at all. Suits. Just coming to talk with the dirt ball."

"Holy crap."

"Yeah, I know. So I says to him, no I don't have my service weapon on me. He asks me to turn around and so I take my Glock out of my waist and show him I laid it on the passenger seat."

"NO YOU DIDN'T."

"Well, yeah, I did. But Kel, the talks were going great. He saw that we saw enough and could arrest him on the spot. But he starts opening up about all this other crap, and Danson starts interrogating him. We've got a boatload of crap on him when all of a sudden he whips out this huge pistol and slams it down on the table. Now he's got us."

"Crap, lieutenant."

"Yeah, me too. All down my shorts. Anyhow, my pager goes off. I don't even know who paged me for what. I ask him if I can use his phone to call and acknowledge the page. He agreed as long as I stood there and talked. That's why I was glad it was you and you picked up on what was going on right away."

I breathe deeply and exhale while he is filling me in. I cannot believe what we just went through together. I won't think about the "what ifs" until later. I try to change the subject.

"Well, thanks for filling me in. And I say next time the guy is doing that to cats, go ahead and shoot first."

"Yeah, me too. It was awful ugly. But thanks again, Kelly, I mean it."

"Yeah, I hear ya. I gotta go now and fill in my staff before they think I've lost my mind."

I hang up with the lieutenant and fill in everyone else as to what happened. They get mad like me and ask all of the same questions that I did. We play the "what if" game a lot. It makes us feel better. I let them learn from my experience. I let them share in the frustration. Then they tell me how freaked out they got because I was in a place where they couldn't reach me. I don't understand at first. I guess I have never imagined it from our side of the radio. We are always trained to use our voices, our words, our tone when we dispatch and direct our guys. We have to, to keep them from getting tunnel vision. I just never imagined it could happen to me. I think back about how alone I felt trying to rescue these guys from a bad place. I am glad it turned out the way it did. If I were to "what if" it now, I would have to say that my entire team would not have been able to jump in and help me if I needed it. And likewise, if I was that closed off to them, what else might I have missed? What else might I have misinterpreted or relayed?

I know this much. I was the one that got that call for help. I had never been coached or trained on the effects of tunnel vision. I didn't know what I could have done wrong. So I followed my guts. Joe once told me I had good guts. I guess this is what he meant. That night, on the way home, I sob uncontrollably with the most extreme case of "what ifs" that I've ever imagined. I get to thinking; I could have messed up so huge that it cost several lives. Then I remember something. That's what I do for a living. We live vicariously through the lives of others.

After a few shifts, it wasn't so scary to pick up the phone again. It was tough at first. I told my squad that I didn't want to talk with the lieutenant even if he asked for me. I was pretty torn about the whole thing. They let me vegetate in my corner. They pretty much ran very little by me. They let me have my space and they coaxed me back into the routine after a while. I knew that as their leader, I had to rebound and make a good example of this ugly situation. I listened more closely to my dispatchers. I watched for signs of tunnel vision or other signs of stress and struggle. I was hypersensitive now, and I made them all a little jumpy. Webster's said to "vicariously experience the feelings, thoughts, and experience of another of either the past or present without having the feelings, thoughts, and experience fully communicated in an objectively explicit manner."

At this stage in my life, I really wanted to learn more in order to help more. I wanted to be smarter, more knowledgeable about communication and how it works. I needed more words, more examples, and more explanations of how to communicate better. Working with my squad, I owed it to them to make myself the best supervisor I could be, and that meant becoming more educated. As I went back to school and filled my mind with the whys and hows of communication theories, I discovered the basics of send and receive communications. I soaked it all in and even ventured into some of the works of the great philosophers. I wondered if

88

the great orators knew that as they stood or sat in the middle of the town square and pondered the meaning of life with all who were within earshot, that they would become my communication models. Likewise, I wondered if they could ever imagine a day when a person spoke through a tube that broadcast voice into billions of little sound bits across the atmosphere. Why should I be any different? I would bore my dispatchers to death with theories and ideas such as these. I would tire them with the possibilities of controlling and persuading the responders in the field with our mere voices and sounds. I needed to know how we as a professional group of dispatchers, call-takers, telecommunicators, and such could use our technology and our voices and our knowledge to help those who call us for help. I wanted to know how and why we could use our words to make good things happen, and how to prevent the bad things from happening. This meant from all who call us on the phone and the radio. It included the good guys, the victims, and anyone else who needed assistance in a matter of seconds. After all else, this is why we are here. I think my partner Joe is proud that I am finally getting the hang of this job.

Love

I never thought I could ever love a job more than I loved my job at age sixteen down at the local Dairy Queen. I could make the perfect little Q on the top of the ice cream cone and I loved it. I wasn't a perfectionist, so this was a huge thing for me to get it perfect every time. I got in trouble at first for dumping the cones and starting over; something about the profit margin being affected. I didn't get it. But I did get the excitement of that little child as they looked at that perfect Q. I imagined they wanted to grow up and be just like me some day.

Then I found 9-1-1. Or it found me. It was nothing like they reported it would be. We had troubles with the radio equipment; the phones would have issues now and then and time after time. We were given reasons wrapped up in an excuse called weather, or sunspots, or atmospheric conditions. These were serious issues. The radios were really bad some nights. The guys' traffic to us would be so covered with "skip" that we couldn't understand if it was them calling us or not. We would muddle through it all night with multiple transmissions of "repeat your last," only to get the same gobbledy-gook. The CAD system would go down for its usual maintenance and the fog would make weird things happen with our radio repeaters which made it sound like aliens invaded our system. This was pretty much the norm everywhere, they told me. I didn't know anything about resources yet. I really didn't know much about APCO (Association of Public Safety Communications Officials) or NENA (National Emergency Number Association).

After all of my formal schooling, I was about to become immersed in these trade organizations.

One of the joys and yet difficulties of being a supervisor is that I am no longer considered one of the gang. I don't really belong on administration's side, but neither do I belong on the side of the dispatchers when they go out to party and relieve stress. It can be a thankless job in that you seem to never really reap any benefits. Once in a while the assistant director or director might throw you a bone and tell you good job. It isn't the same as getting together with others at conferences and finding out that you must be really okay at what you do. Becoming a supervisor is a plus because of being able to facilitate fixes for the dispatch operation. It can be a minus in that the dispatchers do not see how much or what I have to go through to get that fix.

I didn't start out as a shift supervisor because of how much of a leader I was necessarily. I was promoted, finally, because I stood out in the dispatch center. I stood out because I cared about my coworkers, the responders, the citizens, and the job as a whole. I got along well with others. I didn't sound off too much to the boss. I learned how to keep quiet when need be. I hadn't been exposed to any additional leadership training so I wasn't sure if I was in touch, doing the right thing, or even if I was on the right track. I kept listening to my dispatchers as to what they wanted and needed and passed that along to my bosses in the hopes of making a difference. Apparently something worked. I reminded my dispatchers relentlessly that someday they would have to be ready to replace me. They laughed. I told them that "someday when I'm director," they would have to be ready to step up. They laughed again. A few decided to take me up on my plan and rise to the challenge. I like to think I made a noticeable difference in their lives. I coached them (before I knew that's what it was called). I helped them understand the mechanics of people, when to step in, when not. I aided them in their quest to learn more.

Then one lucky summer day in 2001, I arrived at work and received mail. The letter was addressed to me, from APCO. I wasn't even a member. It said for the state of Michigan, for 2001, I was nominated and selected as Supervisor of the Year. I could not believe it. It couldn't be true. I went to my deputy director and asked her if it was a joke. She confirmed it was indeed true and said she would see to it that I had the time off on the schedule to attend the state awards dinner. I was in shock. I read the nomination letter enclosed. I was more in disbelief. I really didn't feel like I knew what I was doing most of the time. Perhaps I helped in a lot of little ways. The awards dinner was held in October of 2001. It was six weeks after the terror and heartache of the September 11 attack on the United States. As I stood at the podium listening to the words of what my staff thought of me and how much I had made a difference in their lives, I could only imagine what the folks at those other dispatch centers must be going through. I hoped they had as supportive of a team as I had. I hoped they were being listened to. I hoped someone cared. I accepted my award with the promise and determination even more grounded to become a 9-1-1 director and make a difference for 9-1-1. I became a member of APCO that week also, and it has opened my eyes immensely. I never knew there was a world of "us" out there. Now that I know it, I will share it even more with my dispatchers. One of the first debates with administration was to allow Internet use in the center. It opened a new world of research and fact finding about how others worked in 9-1-1 centers across the world. It was the best resource yet, in addition to attending classes and conferences. I love being there for my people.

I love the job for what it brings to me. I try to top that with what I bring to the job. The lieutenant stopped by later on to thank me again in person for saving his butt. I asked him to thank my dispatchers since they do it on a daily basis for all of his road guys. He did. The job, the equipment, the glitches, the human side of the job are all lumped together as this job I fell in love with.

Late one evening, I answer the call when all my dispatchers

are tied up.

"9-1-1."

"Oh my god you've got to help me! I can't find my kids!"

The man is screaming all of his words together over and over. My heart breaks in half.

"What do you mean, sir?"

I look at the ANI/ALI screen for the location. It isn't there. Nothing. It comes in with zeros in the number blanks. I can't capture the data and I begin to panic.

"Sir, tell me where you are!" I command him with every authoritative syllable I can muster.

Ohmygoddddd, where is she? Where are they? Ohhhhhhhhhgoddddddddddd."

His agonizing screams are not helping. And he doesn't know that I don't know where he is yet.

"Sir, what's your name?"

"Tom."

"Tom." I lower my voice to almost a whisper as I state with instruction, "Tell me your exact address."

He calms down to tell me it is a trailer park. Then he "re-freaks," as we call it in the industry.

"Ohhhhhhhh, can you help me, pleeeeeeease."

"Tom, I need your numbers."

He gives me his phone number.

"Tom, I'm trying to help you. What are the numbers to your trailer?"

I keep prodding him for the exact location. My awesome dispatcher at police radio has taken his name and is looking for all of the "Toms" in our database in one of two trailer parks with that phone prefix. It is work. I continue my conversation with Tom.

"Tom, I have your phone number. I need the numbers on your trailer so I can help you find your kids."

I hear wailing and moaning as he falls to the floor. He's clutching the phone to him as I hear it scuffle about his body. I see him in my mind's eye crouched down onto the floor somewhere. I

94

try to see what he sees.

"It's her, and she's deaaaaaaad. Ohmygod she's dead. She is in the tub in a pool of blood. Ohgoddd help me!"

He's screaming from the bathroom floor in his trailer while he looks at his wife immersed in a tub full of blood. I cannot imagine the horror. But I must.

"Tom, are you sure she is dead?" I ask calmly but sternly.

"Yes, oh yes, she's gone."

Then it dawns on him.

"MY KIDS, ohmygod MY KIDS, where are my kids?"

Now he's wailing and my dispatcher sends me an electronic message asking me if he's Tom Wasson or Tom Mears.

I must have looked relieved.

"Tom," I shout at him to get his attention momentarily, "is your last name Mears?"

"Yes, ohmygod my kids, where, where, where are my kids?"

He's running through the house looking for his kids. I hear doors being banged open while he frantically scans each room. My staff has acted on the affirmative response about the name. Now we have the exact address and lot number based on a recent trip to this guy's address. They get the ambulance going and all of the officers necessary. Since we haven't found the kids yet, and we didn't know the mindset of this man, they also alert the command officer that it might be a crime scene, too.

"Tom, you're in lot 223, correct?" I confirm one more piece of information, just in case.

"Yeah, 223, and I found a note. It says, ohmygod, it says…"

I almost fall out of my chair.

"Her brother, her brother has the kids…oh my god, thank god."

He's clearly spent, but he's still in a huge state of shock. I remind him that I am with him. "Tom, is there anyone I can call?"

"No, I'll call her brother after I clean up the mess."

"Okay, I have help on the way. I'm sorry, Tom."

"I'm sorry too. I've got three kids. She was the love of my life. Oh god why did she have to do this?"

"I don't know, Tom. There will be a lot of unanswered questions for a while. What ages are your kids?"

We make small talk to keep him occupied. He wonders aloud if he should go back and be with her. I advise him it's not a good thing. He needs to help me think about what to tell the kids. We hear the sirens arrive and I tell him it's okay to hang up. He heaves and sobs heavily while he disconnects.

I do not know what makes people so depressed that they end their life. I have studied some suicidal statistics and facts and theories. I do know that in the majority of cases, they really don't want to die. They want to get rid of the pain. They want to escape from something. It is a last cry. We hear it from our end of the phone and attempt to make sense of it for them. We listen, we empathize, and we share what little sense we can make of this life and why we love it so. Most of the time, the call to 9-1-1 is timely because they know they will get some kind of help. Sometimes, it doesn't happen this way. They call for notification purposes beforehand. They want us to know where to find the body. They want us to clean up the mess before their loved ones discover them. Or at least they try.

"9-1-1."

"We need someone over here to help us, please."

It's Thanksgiving and I just sat down with my shift to enjoy the turkey and stuffing. Hank brought in his deep fryer and promised the shift that it will be the best turkey we've ever eaten in our lives. Mine was going to be cold.

"What's the address where you're calling from?"

"It's my father's house. He was seventy-eight. He left us a note. His dog is dead beside him on the tarp in the living room."

Crap.

"You're the son, you say? What's your name?"

"Steven. We couldn't figure out why he was so late for dinner. He still had all of his wits about him and he's only a mile down the

96

road. We were watching for him to drive to our house for dinner. I can't believe he did it this way."

"You say you know for sure that he is dead?"

"Yes, ma'am. That I am sure of."

"Okay, we have help on the way. Is there anything else I can do for you?"

"No, I will call the others to let them know we will be awhile."

"Okay, Steven, I'm sorry for your loss."

"Thank you."

Life is so matter of fact for us sometimes. We don't understand it. Yet we revel in saving it, bringing it into this world, and hopefully making it better. Nobody ever said it would be so damn difficult. My turkey had to be nuked. It was a little tough to swallow after that.

One of the most memorable events a dispatcher can have is the chance to bring a baby into this world. It is an amazing thing to be a part of.

"9-1-1."

"Come quick, my sister is having a baby NOW!"

"What's the address?"

"A-a-i-i-i-i-e-e-e-e-e, god I dunno. Oh oh oh oh, what's your address?" she asks her sister who I hear is in labor in the background. I hear her doing her breathing exercises. We get the address in between contractions. Clearly, the sister calling has never had, nor witnessed a child being born. The sister in labor, on the other hand, is not new to this. She is having her fourth child and she is only twenty years old.

"A-a-a-a-a-a-a-i-i-i-i-ie-e-e-e-e-e, ohhhhhhh, ahhhhhhhhh," my caller shrieks over and over. I can see her dancing with the phone. I picture her jumping up and down with each scream of nervous energy. It pierces my ear through the headset ear piece. I ask her to calm down so we might help her sister. This puts her over the top. I hear from the woman in labor that the caller needs to stop and help.

"Is she having the baby now?"

"Yes, I told you." She screams again and jumps up and down.

"Can you look and be sure? Listen to me, if the baby is coming, we need to catch it!"

"LOOK? DOWN THERE? Ohmygod NO! I can't look! That's just not right. Oh-oh-oh-oh, a-a-a-a-a-i-i-i-i-e-e-e-e-e, oh-oh-oh."

I hear the sister in labor panting, "It's coming, help me."

I scream back at the caller and tell her to shut up and do as I tell her for the baby's sake.

"Put your hand down there against the opening to apply firm pressure so the baby doesn't come out too fast. DO IT NOW!"

Somehow she does it. I imagine with eyes closed. Likewise, I hear the medics enter the house and tell her to move her hand, they have it now. The phone disconnects.

Sometimes you hear about a dispatcher who brings life into this world. The media plays the call on the nightly news, and they show the dispatcher and the mother connecting either at the center or at the home. It's a pleasant perk of the job. The paramedics have always arrived just in time on my calls. They take over, make the delivery. All is well. I have never personally heard the baby being born. After two decades of almost delivering a baby, it is exciting to hear others work a delivery only to hear the wail of a newborn on the other end of the phone. It's warm and tingly. You hear that little life enter this world kicking and screaming. Once you confirm that everyone is okay, you just know that the baby is going to grow up and be a dispatcher or something cool like that. I, still, love this job.

PART III

As time goes on, we all must grow. We either grow in place with very deep roots, or we grow outwards toward our goals and our resolve.

Resolve

I looked long and hard at my opportunities. I could sit on endless night shifts and read entertainment magazines, or even trade magazines of which I am now a member. A person can only read those so many times. I even wrote an article for the state newsletter for one of the trade organizations. It was about chairs. It was a silly thing really. I've never been one to understand the ferociousness of fighting over chairs in the center. It happens. Most people would never understand how constraining it is to sit for eight, ten, twelve, or even sixteen hours in a chair that doesn't fit right. I liken it to an underworld of negotiations, power, and trickery in order to have your chair at the onset of each shift. Seriously though, aside from all of the shenanigans in the center, I reminded my colleagues, often, that I was hungry for more knowledge. I wanted to make a difference. I was working my way through school and I knew there had to be a bigger way to make a difference for my dispatch staff. Sometimes I would work through the night for my eight hours, get off duty to drive to the community college, and sleep for an hour in my car. Then I would sit through a few classes, run through a fast food drive-thru, and respond back to work for the afternoon shift. I would work those afternoon eight hours and only then go home to get some sleep. As I look back on it I am glad of two things. One is that I never drove stupid, because a lack of sleep can make you do dumb things. Number two is that I never let my school schedule interfere with my work schedule. I always remembered that I had people in the chair counting on me.

A person understands that even better as you move up the chain of command. The smaller the group of people depending on you, the more you affect their lives, either positively or adversely. You realize quickly that you will do anything in the world for them, because some day you will need them to reciprocate. I didn't understand this as a dispatcher because there was always someone hungry enough for the overtime. At least, that's how it was at first. The truth of the matter is that someone has to be there. Someone has to answer the call. If not us, then WHO will it be?

I worked on my degrees steadily. I reminded my wonderful dispatchers that they now have "good guts" and they do an awesome job. Sometimes I mess with their minds and tell them they can pretend to be the supervisor for a while, so I can dispatch again. I miss the road officers. I like telling them where to go. They respond likewise to hearing my voice on police radio. We joke around a bit because it is good to remind my dispatchers that it's okay to be human.

"Car 32, copy a complaint," I radio one of the guys.

"Can it hold, dispatch? I was about to grab a bite to eat."

"10-4, I'll send 31." I give in because I like the road guys too.

"Uh, dispatch, he was going to get a bite with me..." Long pause.

"Okay, you two go eat and I'll hold all heinous crimes for later when you are done eating."

The phones start to ring. Some of them are officers trying to cover for them; a couple of them are sergeants. asking if I was for real. I joke with them and tell them that I'll set it straight on the air. I was playing along with their silliness. Nobody in "scanner land" wants to hear that their complaints have just been put on hold. Nobody wants to imagine that it might take thirty minutes for an officer to come to file a report because he or she hasn't eaten that day. The truth is that most of them wind up eating horribly at greasy spoons or at drive-thrus. The food they ingest in a hurry is not what I would call sitting down to a real meal. They order and hold their breath waiting for the voice on the radio to call out their number. I know what they say about dispatch. I've ridden along. I've been hungry right alongside them. I know they get a little grumpy if they haven't eaten. I know that they don't mean to bite our heads off. I try to convey that to my dispatchers as I remind them that cops are human too. My police dispatcher doesn't want to let me dispatch his cops anymore. He kicks me out of the chair.

The opening for an assistant director for a different dispatch center wasn't even on my radar. I was told about it from others. They insisted that I would be perfect. I hadn't imagined that I would be ready. I was scared to death because it was with a whole different center in a whole new place. What would they think of me? How would I get to know their practices, their geography, their cops, or even them? Would they know how much I've given to my dispatchers here as a shift supervisor? Would they care? So many questions and I hadn't even filled out the application yet. If I was ever going to be a director someday this would be the next logical step. I filled out the application and sent it in the mail while my stomach danced full of butterflies. Then I got the call to come for an interview. I got an interview. I made the list. I didn't know what to think. My mind was racing with all kinds of voices, questions, and "what-ifs."

I visit the center after the first interview. I ask the dispatch supervisor on duty a question. I ask what she would change. Other than expanding the already beautiful center, there wasn't much she would change. Could it be this easy? Could it be this wonderful? I ask myself over and over what I might have answered if someone would have asked me that question at different stages of my career. I am offered the position of assistant director a few weeks later. I am determined to make this happen because after all, I've stayed the course to resolve to make things better for dispatch. This is finally my chance. I start out slowly. My boss is an established, respected, and revered director. He leads by example. He sets the course and is admired by others in the industry. My staff tells me that he does all of this without paying attention to them. I see things. I see differences of opinion. I am trying to understand. I look around and see wonderful things. The center is finely built and everything has been thought of with the limited budget he has under his domain. I watch and learn. It is his intention to groom me to take his position. Can this be true? Finally, I will see the day when I am a director? I must concentrate on the assistant director position first. This is a lot of work.

To begin in my new role, I arrive at seven in the morning or there 'bouts. I am there until nine or ten or eleven sometimes at night. I have a lot to learn. I learn all of my dispatchers' and supervisors' names and I know about their families somewhat. I meet new deputies and other officers. I start to attend meetings, and more meetings, and even more meetings. I have committees to answer to. At least my boss does, and I have to know how to run them when he is gone. I hear how much he knows and how far the center has come. He makes statements that I will pick up and maintain a wonderful center. They question. The fire chiefs, police chiefs, and lieutenants and captains wonder about me, and from where I've come. We give reports to commissioners and attend nighttime meetings with township officials and citizens.

My boss, the director, makes his announcement that he is going to retire and I will hopefully replace him. Every time I hear him, I have doubts, or fear, maybe. I work harder at proving myself. I study the names, the positions, the departments, and whether or not they have valid complaints. I then check with my boss and he explains that we cannot do anything to fix it. There are reasons. I slowly start to see and understand. I want my dispatch staff to get this. They aren't exposed to these meetings and surely they don't hear how much my boss is going to bat for them. There are reasons why he cannot change the computer to do what the fire department wants and make it work as easily for the dispatchers to use while dispatching the call.

There are vendors, salespeople, and others to answer to. Then there is the community of other 9-1-1 directors and assistant directors. Thank the universe! These people know stuff. They've been there, done that, and then share and compare notes. That's good to know. I will need them plenty after he is gone. I resolve myself to a commitment towards obtaining the director's position, so I work harder, longer.

I listen to my dispatchers complain about each other and about the officers and the firefighters and paramedics.

"What's going on here?" I ask.

I interview my supervisors and ask them what needs to be changed. They are at a loss. They want me to change things, but do not know what they want; or more importantly, what they want changed. I start sending them out to other places, other training, and other centers. I have them attend conferences. They come back armed with knowledge.

"Oh, what have I done?" I think to myself.

We work together to institute a new medical dispatch protocol. This takes community effort and participation from yet another subcommittee of participants. Then there is the schedule. I swear it will be the only reason my hair turns pure white. I cannot imagine how people in administrative positions get anything done when you have to pay so much attention to the schedule. There are vacations to query, post, and fill. There are two rounds where people make their first and second vacation picks known. I fill out the year with the proposals and make sure everyone can get their time off. That was one of the things I knew I would change if/ when I had the chance. Only I think sometimes I am making more of a mess than when I got here. The good part is that it makes my supervisors step up and be more accountable as well. They have to help if they want me to make it to the director's position; I cannot do everything. They step up. They help a ton. I sure appreciate them, and they know it. They learn more about me. Equally, I learn their ways and how to better support them.

"I need you to know that I am impressed with what you have

done so far for us," Supervisor Nela tells me in my office late one night.

"Thank you," I reply.

"But I want you to know more about me and how I think you can help me," she continues.

"Okay, let me hear what you have." I encourage her even though it is going on seven and I have already been here twelve hours. I am excited to hear more about my night shift supervisor.

"I was nominated once for supervisor of the year also. I have always run my shift top notch." Then comes her concern. "You don't seem to be understanding my struggles with these new young men on nights."

"Okay, explain."

"Well, I want them to do things my way on my shift. I am not going to change and do things their way."

"Can you give me some examples?"

We go back and forth for the next two hours about her leadership style. She is taking notes and soaking up everything I say. She says things like, "I've never thought of it that way," and "Well, I guess I can see it from their point of view." I know I am getting through to her as well as answering her questions about my vision for this department. We do plenty of brainstorming that night and for many more nights after that. Trust is a two-way street, as is respect.

An assistant director has to continue to play the middle man. It is apparent that the position must support the director. It is hard to be there for the staff and still walk that fine line. I worked diligently to prove that I could become the director once my boss was ready to retire. He told everyone he would be ready in three to five years. I figured I had lots of time to learn. I buckled down to take it all in. I sat in dispatch to try to learn how my staff puts calls into the computer. It was the same, but different. The template was different but the commands were the same. I spent time learning the policies and procedures, the union contracts, the cops and their jurisdictions and car numbers. I had to spend a lot of time with people. I wanted to believe them for who they were, not who I was told they were. I formed my own opinions. I believed in them with a clean slate one and all. I wanted them to start over with me as I would be starting with them. I sent them to training. I learned their schedules and tried to keep track. While learning all about them, I was studying to become the next director. I loved it, and I was on my way finally. I resolved to be the best assistant director, and I was on my way to fulfilling my goal of becoming the best 9-1-1 director, too. I would get there. I could feel it. I was now making a difference in the lives of my new dispatch center. As a part of reaching my goals laid out before me, I was setting examples for my staff back at my former center. I missed them tremendously.

Some of the job duties of the assistant director were clearly related to hiring and firing people. The hiring part was absolutely more fun. I loved hiring people. I got a kick out of offering them the job. They were as tickled to become a dispatcher as I was at becoming the assistant director. I call one of them.

"Cami, this is Kelly at the dispatch center."

"Yes?"

"Are you still interested in a job with us?"

"Yes?!"

"Okay, because we are still interested in you."

"Okay?!"

"So, do you want to work for our dispatch center?"

"YES!!!"

"For the rest of your life?" I tease.

"Absolutely!!" She is thrilled. She would say whatever she needed to at this point.

Working as a 9-1-1 dispatcher is the most thrilling, exciting, phenomenal job I have ever known. I have worked in factories, at fast food restaurants, in sales, and in a variety of other jobs. There is a fascination about answering the call and dispatching the call. It takes a rare person to handle it all the way through. There is no training that can prepare you for what the gunshot sounds like when it actually happens in your ear. There is no describing the exact way someone sounds when they are dead and their body is breathing only because the brain is telling it to long after the heart has stopped. When someone thinks they can do this job, they come in full of resolve and anticipation. They believe us when we train them along the way. They trust us not to take off the training wheels too soon. Our training program is now nine months long with an additional three months of a shadow phase. After a year, one barely understands the full capacity of what powers they have. We watch them carefully. It is only after approximately three years that they truly get it. By then, they either get out, or they stay for the long haul. There are those that don't make it through the first year, of course. They wash out fairly often. You cannot sit in the center and say to yourself, "That sounds easy, I can do this job." It looks easy because the folks taking those calls have had thousands of calls practicing the job. The more senior dispatchers practice by taking barking dog complaints. They learn to dig deeper for the truth. They learn to trust when the hair on the back of their neck stands up. They pick up on key words and background noises. We have no solid training outside of the center that teaches us how to make all of this make sense. There really isn't any formal training that helps you figure it out. Yet!

Life is an interesting teacher. We all learn as much as we can from others so that we don't make their mistakes along with our own. As assistant director, it is a tough arena. It isn't what I thought it would be. I cannot tell them everything. I liken it to raising kids. Sometimes I have to deliver notice that I cannot explain, similar to telling a child not to play with matches. How do you show them the consequences in complete honesty? I cannot explain why I have to deliver a policy that looks unfair. It might seem that way. It has that look or feel to it. It isn't meant to be unfair. It really is for the good of how you do the job. It will protect you, trust me. I seem to be very far away from taking the call. I miss the camaraderie sometimes. There are reasons why the resolve appears to blur.

I have a lot more meetings to attend nowadays. I cannot seem to focus on the schedule as much as I need. I feel for my staff. They are trying to put things in perspective but this is their time off; their lives that I have responsibility over. My staff is feeling like I've let them down. There are vacancies, or positions not filled that need to be filled. People are doing a lot of overtime. There is so much to take care of in order to take care of them. I need to call a fire chief; he thinks one of my dispatchers was sassy on the air. I listen to the tape first. It was not as he described. Of course, I find out upon speaking with him that he heard it third hand. The firefighter on the other end of the radio was half asleep and was trying to cover his butt for taking an enormous amount of time to respond to the call. Either way, I feel like I spend a lot of time chasing my tail. The radios are really bad this spring. The dispatchers are dealing with a lot of stress. I can feel it. I stay late. Sometimes I feel as though I have gone back in time. I am now working more than twelve hours in a day. I have meeting after meeting with this committee and that one. They all want to have a say in how dispatch is run. They are supposed to have oversight and we confer with them about policy and procedure. We ask them for little in return and we consistently hear complaints at the meetings. I ask them if they have my number and ask them to call me when the supposed infraction occurs. I don't want to hear about it months later at a meeting. I explain to them the training process and the hiring process and ask them to sit in dispatch to see how it has changed.

A police chief calls to complain. He is insistent that he has been wronged by one of my staff. I ask him to come see me. At first he says he wants a copy of the tape. I get the tape and listen to it over and over. I am incensed because he was the one in error attempting to put a dispatcher in her place. As I go over the tape, I hear more in the way he says what he is saying, and my dispatcher is reacting the only way she can to save face. I am interrupted by a dispatcher asking if she can talk with me. She wants to quit.

She says she has had enough. The time has come. She appreciates all that we have given her but her time has come and she will be leaving today. I receive her letter of resignation stated simply in one sentence, "I quit." The police chief arrives and is outside my door. She leaves and he comes in as I answer the phone from human resources. Union negotiations are tomorrow and I need to bring over a couple of things pertaining to the schedule and the hiring process when I come over. I agree.

"How's your day, Chief?"

"Better than yours apparently," he states matter-of-factly and correctly, I bet.

"Well, I've listened to the tape, and I'd like you to listen as well," I tell him.

"I don't need to hear it. I know that we are a small town police department, but I expect to get the same kind of service as the larger departments. I am told that you will make changes and I am here to ask that you look into doing this." He doesn't miss a beat.

"Well, I am glad that we are of the same mind-set. Let's have a listen for a minute."

I play the tape. He basically sounds like a silly fool yelling at my dispatchers on the radio. Then he follows up with a phone call that is even more ridiculous at three in the morning. He looks at me with a stunned look. He tries to play it off by a slight shrug of his shoulders.

"JERK."

I don't know what comes over me. I think it is a knee-jerk thing after listening to the tape again and finally looking him in the eye. After all, my dispatchers were only trying to preserve his safety.

"Well, if you are accusing me of being a jerk, then point taken," he says stoically.

"Yessir, that's exactly what I am saying. You were a jerk! I think you hear and see what I do, and there is little I can do to defend you or your position. As far as my dispatcher, I think she deserves a medal. In addition to just having done CPR on a little old lady with the husband, she gets your radio and phone traffic and handles your incident professionally. Then she goes on to take a B&E in progress without missing a beat. I need to recommend her for dispatcher of the year. She never even mentioned to the supervisor or to me that you were a jerk. I came to that conclusion on my own."

"Well, yes, I see."

"You are welcome to the tape. I am not going to reprimand my dispatcher."

"That's okay. While I am here, I wanted to talk with you about some other issues though."

We move on to other topics, other items of discussion. He leaves the tape on my desk when he goes. I throw it in a drawer for future. I like to be right and my dispatchers are right just about all of the time. I know this from experience. The tape always covers our butts. We live and die by it from our professional standards. The chief just forgot he was talking to a former dispatcher with resolve to make things right all the way around. As a side note, had my dispatcher been in the wrong, I am sure she would have mentioned it to her supervisor, who would have mentioned it to me, to give me a heads up that it was coming. Furthermore, the supervisor and I did talk about the tape, the call, the entire incident to make sure the dispatcher would know how to get out of a situation like that in the future. This would ensure that she did not lose her nerve or let a situation get the best of her, detracting her from delivering stellar officer safety and customer service.

So much to learn. So much to know. So much to be responsible for. I call them my dispatchers. I refer to them still as my family, my people. I defend them vigorously and talk about them proudly. I am making it in this role of assistant director. Apparently I am making a name for myself. I am becoming what I always dreamed. I am able to make a difference for them. They answer the call now. They listen, they live for the job, and they dispatch the calls with all the right tools. I am responsible for getting them the tools. I coach the supervisors so they can coach the dispatchers. I help them with the people issues so they can help the dispatchers deal with the calls. It's not all textbook. You never know what or why or how the job will get to some. They don't always know how to tell you. My supervisors are a great bunch. They see the light. They learn more and more. They are like sponges and they are in charge of making sure the center hums. It is an awesome place to be. I love my job. I am making a difference for all of them. I also see that next step looming. Am I ready?

I tidy up things in the assistant director position. I set the standards for what I want to accomplish. I work on the rapport between the road and my staff. I know this is pivotal. One morning, I have had enough of the ranting on one particular shift. I make a request of the road sergeant. The next day I have relief in the center for the entire day shift squad. They want to know what is going on. I move them all into a conference room, where they meet face to face, eye to eye, knee to knee, and elbow to elbow with the very same road guys that they dispatch. They all squeeze into this small conference room and they look at me with less than kindness in their eyes. They must be thinking something like, "Crazy lady." I smile big at them.

"You are all here at the request of me and your sergeant. We are going to get to the bottom of things with you all face to face. It is time to get back to what we do and why we do it. If you have a problem with it, now is the time to air it. Otherwise, by the time we leave this room, you will all have a clear picture of doing the job and taking the personal crap out of it. Got it?"

It is one of the weirdest moments I've ever had (next to rolling on the floor with that deputy). In a way, this is group verbal fisticuffs. I've asked them to take off the boxing gloves and talk to each other as real persons, not just voices on the radio. We discover a lot about each other. I see my dispatchers start out tight-lipped and nervous and become open and curious. I see the deputies with their arms crossed, eyes turned down, and not wanting to open

112

up, eventually explain why they were so upset with the way they were dispatched. Silly things and still they are important things when you consider all of the officer safety issues. Again, we never know how much we mean to each other unless we take a moment to walk in the other's shoes. It opens up the entire room. Pretty soon there are smiles replacing frowns, and relaxed shoulders, and crossed legs with uncrossed arms. We laugh, we joke, and we make silly promises. We walk out of there knowing that we are all in this together. One of the deputies pulls me aside as I exit the conference room.

"I know what you're up to."

"Excuse me?"

"I see it, and you know what?"

"What?"

"It's going to work."

He's grinning wildly and I stop to look him squarely in the eye.

"What do you think I'm trying to accomplish here?"

"Well, I know for a fact that you want us all to just get along and understand that we're all human and we need each other. I think it is brilliant. I know this will work because it is what we have needed for a very long time. I just want you to know that I thank you."

"Wow! Okay, thank you!"

He shakes my hand firmly and asks when I will do a ride-along with him sometime. I promise soon. We promise each other to continue to work on communications as a whole.

Trust

Upon building trust with all of the police, fire, and EMS departments, as well as within my own center, I start to feel grounded. I buy a house that is around the corner from my center. This is a good thing, I think. I can live and grow and be there for my staff in person as well as through phone and electronic means. I am now putting in twelve-hour days routinely because I am trying to keep up with my assistant director job while working my way up to director. It is okay with me, though, because I know this cannot last. I will get the hang of things and they will slow down, I am sure. I begin to get the hang of all of my committees and boards and people I answer to. Then I branch out to the other agencies and the organizations that enable us to learn and grow with future vision. I start to see things as they will be or as they should be. I learn quickly how we need to be able to communicate all around our communities better and learn how to do things cooperatively.

This is about the time the push was on for interoperable communications. Nationally, people were responding to calls into areas where they can't talk to one another. It is as if September 11 was finally trickling down. We all know we aren't on our own little island. Now the government wants to make sure of it. I hear it from my fire chiefs, my police chiefs, and from everyone else. They want more money, more radios, and more interoperability. They want the dispatch radio system to be more for all of them, and be better for all of us. They want better equipment and better ways to communicate. We put our heads together and research our options. With the 9-1-1 money, we purchase and maintain more radio equipment and mobile computers so we can use other ways and means to communicate with officers and firefighters. We need to relay alleged incidents of hazardous materials, suspicious substances, terrorist sightings, and accurate, or not so accurate, warnings that not every citizen needs to hear necessarily. We have more responsibility heaped upon the dispatchers as to what they can say and how they can say it as well as to whom they can say it. There are laws and ordinances and warnings about what information can be shared, and sometimes there are questions about which way is the best way to disseminate that information.

So, what about the dispatchers? Can't they just do the job anymore? I try to explain to the community how we spend our millage funds responsibly. Some really don't get what we do. Why should they? They trust that we know what we do and that we do it consistently, and they count on us to keep doing it in the event they may ever need us.

"You have to do all that?"

"I thought you just answered the phone."

"I didn't know you had to be trained in all of that."

"I guess I just don't understand what you people do in that 9-1-1 center."

Even our most trusted, faithful politicians, who go to bat for us year after year, asking for the funding to continue because of the importance of keeping our 9-1-1 center up to date, don't know exactly what we do. They admit it. How can they keep up when it is a full-time job for me to try to keep up? I try to help by explaining the little things. I call the news when there are good things to report. I write articles for the local paper to pay tribute to all of our public safety team. I congratulate the officers and firefighters and paramedics because they make all of us look good.

So, what about the dispatchers? Who makes them look good? I try to build them up. I remind them that the second full week of April is National Public Safety Telecommunications Week. I tell them to go to the websites and see what other centers are doing to celebrate. I ask the commissioners for the annual resolution proclaiming the week for "Those who answer the call." It is pretty cool. And they have a lot of fun. We create awards and build enthusiasm for the center because it is about them and the way that they handle doing a tough job. They don't get the spotlight and most of them would rather keep it that way. This is the one time of the year that they need to be spotlighted. We need to remind everyone that what they do is change lives, protect property, and alter the future. They bring life into this world and they escort life out of it. Because of them, the first responders go home the same way they come in every day. It is a tremendous honor to do the job. I am very proud to be able to help them in any way that I can see I make a difference. I trust them to keep doing the job the way they do with all of their heart, and I know that they trust me to keep them safe, and cover their butts.

For the week of the celebration, there is a lot of work that goes into it. I can't imagine what goes on, if anything, in smaller centers where there is only a director and just a handful of dispatchers and such. It is a lot of work to plan a celebration, and ours is a celebration like none other. If you have ever hosted a party where you had to help with the planning, preparation, notification, prizes, awards, ceremony, and such, then you are starting to understand. This should be a celebration and it should be as big or as little as the dispatch staff want it to be. It is about them, after all. I work up the wording for plaques and for certificates. I contact people who do that sort of thing after I get permission from the county to spend our dispatcher fund money for such things. When I was a dispatcher, I would never have understood the process. I have to take into consideration how much my boss has afforded certain line items in the budget for the process. Whether it is for printing of materials, or postage for mailings, or clothing as customary or particular to the job, I must seek approval. If the clothes are for the job or for a special detail like with the cops, then I can make it work. But if it is for prizes for the sake of prizes, then no, it won't be allowed.

I understand the consequences and even get it when I am told we cannot accept donations. I try to put together a party fit for heroes on a limited budget and even less of an understanding. I ask for donations of appreciation and specify that it cannot be monetary. Heck, even if they want to donate to a charity in the name of 9-1-1 it is okay to do that. So much to learn, so much to teach. I try to explain to my dispatchers what is allowed and what is not. Now they see the party as having stipulations. I ask for their help and they ask why they have to host their own party. They are wary of having to do all the work for their own recognition, and, thinking like a dispatcher, I get it. Thinking like an administrator, I feel I must do as much as I can and let the rest go. I hear so often from people I engage with about the job that they have little or no understanding of what goes on in the center. I tell my dispatchers that I am always out there representing you and I ask you to represent all 9-1-1 dispatchers everywhere. There are too many horror stories of how one of us failed, or the system failed one of us and it cost a life. We never want that to happen to any of us. So we hold our heads high and try to do the best we can do at all times. I think that deserves a party.

We throw our party. We invite some of the local agencies to attend; we give out awards and explain what has been happening in the center for the past year. We have made great progress. A lot of the local cops and firefighters even attend to honor those who answer the call. There are plenty of smiles, lots of food, of course, and even a smattering of media folks. There are balloons and videos that the dispatchers have made of themselves and about their center. Those receiving awards will be nominated on a state level to receive recognition and commendation among their peers from across the state. Families are thankful to see their loved ones receive such recognition. It is a fun time and it brings all of us together. We know the job like no one else. It is quirky like that. It is why we trust each other with our own lives.

Back to work. The party is good and lasts for a while. We still have to take the calls. There are people who miss out on the actual awards and party because they are sitting in the center taking the calls. We must be there for each other, even if it means missing each other.

Endurance

The changes in the center do not stop the call load. They might change how it looks, but it doesn't change the fact that the job goes on. The technology of cell phones is the best example. When we took the land line phone calls and knew from where people were calling, we could trust with a fair degree of certainty (although we never would completely) that the call was actually coming from there. Since the cell phone explosion, we still struggle daily with ascertaining where the call is coming from. People learn how to get around the way things work. It defeats the purpose of the location technology. How can we dispatch someone to the location if we never know the location? Even in a state where the technology was advanced by a funding mechanism that promised that dispatch would be able to understand if the cell call was coming in with the coordinates from the cell phone tower location or the cell phone itself was at best confusing. Most dispatchers learn quickly that you have to ask WHERE, WHERE, and WHERE before anything else. We never take it for granted anymore. Even if the cell phone coordinates would be correct with that company or that phone or even that location, the person may have taken that little identification card (SIM card) out of the phone and put it into another, which makes the phone pretty much useless for 9-1-1 purposes. To top that off, the companies that sell "pay as you go" phones don't take into consideration that if you are injured or having a stroke and are unable to tell the dispatcher where you are, then we might never know where you are.

The dispatchers have learned all kinds of tricks to work with the technology as it advances. Will every dispatcher think to look up GPS (global positioning system) coordinates on the Internet and transpose them on a separate mapping system and mimic the coordinates by testing other cell phones in the area and plotting coordinates? There are so many challenges. In a profession whereby everyone demands certain standards because lives are at stake, it is most difficult to keep up. Sharing information and keeping up with that changing knowledge is not limited to 9-1-1. As one can see, though, it is not making things easier for us. For example, if airbags in vehicles must be standardized, they are given ways and means and time to do so. Where is the assistance for 9-1-1? We endure the process of technology and its impact on people without so much as an afterthought of how 9-1-1 will receive that call. People move from one location to another across the state or across the nation and keep their same number. Where will they call when they dial 9-1-1?

As dispatchers try to dispatch resources to aid individuals in everyday emergencies, there are those occasions when even the government forgets how broadly 9-1-1 is impacted. When NASA sends a space shuttle out into space, and it comes back into the atmosphere and explodes, who do people call? And when officials tell people to report suspicious parts or pieces that might be related to that shuttle, who do people call? When there are single or two-person dispatchers in remote areas across the nation still, and they haven't got the technology to determine where you are calling from, how do they handle that call?

As the calls came in on September 11, all of us on the job sat and wondered, "What about the dispatchers?" It was nineteen days before any of us saw the first report on what effects all of that terror had on the dispatchers. NINETEEN days. As assistant director, I know all too well what the effects of remnants of calls rolling around in a person's head can do to them. I know that it is my responsibility to make sure all of my people are okay at all times. During big calls and not so big calls, I keep track of them because it is more than my job. I am proud to take care of the people who answer the call. I help them endure and put up with the demands of the ever-changing job. I try to understand the technology, the changes, and the laws that affect the job daily so that they can concentrate on answering the call. I try to implement policies, procedures, and changes around them to help them do the job easier. All the while, I keep asking myself, "What about the dispatcher?" And I teach them to do the same. I ask them if they've called on our neighbors when we see on the news a tragedy that came through their center. I ask them if they know who took the call, and how is that person doing? I ask them to stand up for one another. That is the only way they will endure a tough time in our center. We must be there for each other. Across the state, across the country, or around the globe, we all must endure the same kinds of stress and the same types of struggles.

We read in the news about a couple of dispatchers who are fired for messing up a call. They are critiqued because of the way the call was handled. Does anyone truly know what happened before, during, or after? As we have learned by listening to the tapes, the dispatchers are usually right. What if they are wrong? What must have happened to have them be so wrong? Did a policy fail? Were there enough resources? Were they trained properly? Was the person not clear in their request? It is still important to remember that human beings make mistakes. We are all too human. That is why it is so remarkable what doesn't make the news every day; the countless calls that are taken whereby lives are saved. Who records them? How do you tally those reports? How do you accurately report or record what a person has done in the course of a day or a month or a year when they potentially save lives every minute? I think it would look like the atomic clock in reverse. Instead of counting down, it would tick off the lives saved as the seconds digitally changed so fast that the red LED numbers are a blur.

The part of Merriam Webster's definition of endurance I like best is the following:

> "the ability to withstand hardship or adversity; especially: the ability to sustain a prolonged stressful effort or activity *a marathon runner's endurance" (Merriam Webster electronic references)

The part about enduring such as sustaining a prolonged stressful effort or activity is very much what a 9-1-1 dispatcher does. They live in a constant marathon. It is with heavy sadness in my heart when I see and hear them eating themselves and working themselves into a state of health that is the extreme opposite of that of a marathon runner.

When will we make a difference? Who will start? How can we endure and make a change if no one will rise up and take care of those who answer the call? In the most ironic terms, I must say that the one who answers the call, dispatches the call, and takes care of the responders and the citizens alike are the very ones who need someone to lift them up and take care of them. It is within this communion that I develop my resolve even further and finally reach my goal. I am promoted to the director's position.

Communion

I started in this profession with the resolve to figure it out (whatever "it" is) and someday become perfect at it. Or at least die trying. I never realized that it was an impossible challenge. If you ever get it perfect or figure it all out, like my coworker Sheila said, then you need to get out of the business. There is no room for complacency. It kills. You never stop learning in any environment or job, especially this one. I know that I promised myself throughout my career that I wanted to grow up and be a director some day. I loved influencing people's decisions, guiding them on their life journey and such. I just never realized all of the learning and growing I would go through as a boss.

I learned things like 1. You are never too old to learn, 2. Positives are harder than negatives, and 3. People who eat at you day in and day out can make you mean. (This is within your own choosing.) And in general, you never quite understand the intricacies of this job. There are always new systems, new radios, new phones, new computers, new methods, and new ideas on how to take the call. We always want to be there to take the call; sometimes we need to be able to exhale and take a moment to ourselves. The technology is changing so rapidly (like in any other job) that it literally blows our minds. We came from the old push button phones that didn't always light up to phones on a computer touch screen. The day is around the corner where you will see the person calling you on a video display just as it shows in the movies. Will dispatch want or need to see that? Should we? How much information can we humanly pass along? And what if we get the video transferred to the responding units? Should they see the assault in progress as they are driving down the road responding to the call? Do we need to see the person being stabbed while they hold the phone in the attacker's face?

There are a gazillion ways to transmit data and voice nowadays. People have no idea that their wireless phone is GPS system based or network based (where it involves triangulation of time and distance of tower sites). Some don't care, some don't ask, and some ask, "What fine print?" They just expect it to work. Like the little old lady who called me a butthead. She expected that I knew things that I really didn't. We can't be as fancy as private industries that have private investors and research and development. We just aren't there. YET! Kids are typing a zillion bits a second on every imaginable device out there and calling it texting. We call it a nightmare when one of them tells us that they got a text message from a "friend" in California that they've never met before who is threatening suicide right now. They call us on an old-fashioned land line. We see the caller is in Michigan. How on earth do we find the kid in California, known only as nen*urfdog127? And when will we receive those infamous text messages into the center from cell phones?

As I explained it to my committee of commissioners, "Someday soon I will need to come back and ask for more personnel. Not because of the number of calls coming in necessarily, but due to the number of ways or devices that will contact 9-1-1. That is where we will need people to dedicate their attention to that method of communication." It blew their hair back!

As a new director I promised a lot of things. Oh, there were lots of little things like a new cabinet for the dispatcher bathroom, a new color for the kitchen walls, a rolling cart for the trainers, and new laptops for the trainers to train with. Then there were things like better radios and updated procedures and better communication between road and dispatch. I jumped in feet first. I had to pick an assistant director that would help me figure things out. This was fortunate because at first I had four from within that wanted to serve alongside me. This was uplifting. One made it all the way through and it was clear we were going to need more time to get ourselves grounded. I couldn't learn my job, teach her hers, and still maintain the relationships that I once had with my dispatchers and supervisors. Another step removed from the communications center for me. How is it that when you are promoted, people just believe that you will figure it out? After all, you were good at what you did before. Clearly you should be able to manage people and still oversee what they do. My assistant director learned boatloads of information quickly. I passed along every piece of knowledge about people skills that I could cram into her brain and she developed the rest of the way. We were starting to click.

When you are a director of anything anywhere, people assume you have the knowledge and the power to control the budget. This translates into being the money person. I never knew how powerful that part was. While it was intimidating at first, I soon gained a lot of experience from other directors and department heads. I also relied on my good ol' bunch of 9-1-1 directors. As many different types and kinds of communication centers as you can imagine, there are that many types of directors and then some. They all have their styles and methods and systems. There were plenty of funding questions and legislative lessons and learning curves to venture down.

The most important thing I did first was to put my systems in place. I knew I needed organization and accountability. I followed what Rudy Giuliani said about all of the drills they had pre-September 11. He said he always drove home the message that they needed to routinely communicate and constantly practice—only he didn't know what he was practicing for exactly. The communication techniques bailed out a lot of people who otherwise wouldn't have known how to put one foot in front of another. I believe in preparedness. I also wanted open lines of communications. So we practiced it!

As time went on, I learned other things from leaders that I took and made my own. As a professor in my undergraduate studies jokingly and not so jokingly said one time, "The best ideas are stolen." Of course in the 9-1-1 directors association, they were always preaching to us to make sure we didn't reinvent the wheel. They were always there to assist and copy and cut and paste to help out. So one day I called on a fellow 9-1-1 director and asked her a question that had been burning in my brain.

"Sally, how did you use that folder system again and what did the colors stand for?"

She laughed and said it could work for whatever I wanted but hers worked like this.

"Red is my budget folder because money matters, blue is for future projects, green is my people friendly file, yellow is my to-do-file, and so on."

It was just an idea, and it worked for her. I put it to use and within a week my desk clutter went away. I could process things in their respective folders as either urgent or important. I learned that I could systematically file my emails the same way. The first lesson I learned as a boss was that while something might seem important, I had to evaluate if it was urgent (or would become urgent). As my predecessor used to say, "What will happen if I do nothing?" Most of the time things had a way of taking care of themselves. I knew this as a dispatcher; why shouldn't it work for me now as a director?

Getting back to the money part, I must say, I've never had so many "friends" who wanted me to look at their product before. To those who helped me find my way, I am forever grateful. Then there were the ones who were already being paid for a product who rarely delivered. This had to end. It takes time to work things out when there are money or damages or discipline involved. It takes people like chiefs and committees and legal representation. It takes resources like documentation, second chances, due process, and the like. It takes time like days and weeks and seasons and even longer.

Then there are the constant questions about why it isn't fixed. I wish I could answer that one. In the world of radio technology it is as crazy as the neighbor's baby monitor making your garage door open and close. It makes as little sense as the neighbor's portable phone talking over your television. And still, the airwaves are becoming more and more compacted than ever before. There is so much riding on the airwaves, it's a wonder we can transmit and receive at all. Think of the number of phones, televisions, and electronic devices in one home in one city or village. Now multiply that by the population in that city or county. So when my consultant told me that there were atmospheric conditions that played a part in all of it as well, I thought my brain would explode. I learned about tropospheric ducting. No kidding. When certain channels or transmissions get stuck in an atmospheric duct (like your furnace) and it drops out of the end of the duct somewhere, it could easily dump into your radio system, thus leaving it immobilized. Holy cow, Batman. This was my introduction to being a new director. I thought I was supposed to be dealing with police and fire and EMS stuff.

Like it or not, I soon became entrenched in learning about radios and signals and transmitters and receivers and simulcast and duplexers and rebanding and narrow banding and everything else that I never before realized happened behind the scenes. All I ever needed or wanted to know as a dispatcher was I selected a button, pushed it, and talked. It was supposed to work a hundred percent of the time. Officer safety, right? Hmmmmm!

I had all kinds of heartburn trying to figure out why things worked or didn't work due to sunspots or ducting or tilt of the earth. My dispatchers were deserving of a better answer than sunspots, for crying out loud. Then I learned about sunspots. Holy crikey, it wasn't just a line. As a director of a communications center, I thought I had heard it all.

One crazed night before Thanksgiving I go into the center because of the ducting and radio issues at three in the morning. As I sit in my office on the phone with the possible perpetrator delivering their data into our voice system, I can't help but overhear a million (or so) phone lines ringing in the center. I make haste and run in to help answer phones. Like riding a bicycle, some things just come to you even after you've been away. As I answer the phones one after another, I hear my supervisor confirming with a township official that the radio waves somehow triggered the tornado warning sirens all over the entire township of some eighty thousand people. They all take turns calling and asking us if there was a tornado on this thirty-nine-degree morning.

"9-1-1, where is your emergency?" I start out official like I hear my staff doing.

"Yes, the sirens just woke me and I was wondering if we are having a tornado?"

"No ma'am, it is a false alarm, thank you for calling."

"9-1-1, where is your emergency?"

"Is there something I should know about? I mean, are we really under a tornado warning?"

"No sir, it is a false trip."

"Well, I thought so, but my wife insisted that I call..." He tries to continue to tell me why he called 9-1-1 and I cut him off to answer the next call in case it is a real emergency. In the meantime, all around me, my staff is doing the same, answering call after call.

"9-1-1." I leave it at that.

"Yeah, I was just woke up by the siren. Is there a storm?"

"No ma'am, it's just time to put the turkey in the oven." I pause. She laughs. I thank her for calling and hang up.

"9-1-1."

"Yeah, is there a tornado?"

"No, it's just time to hit the sales. They're having them on Thanksgiving Day now, you know?" I tease a little.

"Oh? Really?"

"No, just kidding, ma'am, but we don't know why the sirens

are sounding. We assume a false trip; thanks for calling, though."
I end it gracefully because I don't think she got the humor.

After a few more calls, I keep up the rhythm of the "cook the
bird" and "hit the sales" themes. One of my dispatchers takes note
and points it out to the shift supervisor.

"Uh, Jake, did you hear the boss telling people that it's time to
cook the turkey?"

He stares at me with his mouth hung open as if to doubt her
and let me override it. I smile back with a huge grin and remember
my days of "stand by for chest pains" and just leave it at that. For
all of those calls and people calling me names and telling me what
they were going to do about something; for once, it is nice again to
have the upper hand and have a little harmless fun. He is stunned
but forgiving. The rest of the dispatchers think it is pretty cool to
see the boss cut loose a bit. I guess bosses can be human and get
away with it once in a while after all.

Once we wrap up the sirens and imagine all of those people
getting dressed to hit the sales, I remind them of the traffic calls
they are going to start getting. We all laugh and I put the radio
issue to rest while helping my staff have a little fun with a silly
crisis. It was for all the right reasons. We were able to laugh on
that Thanksgiving morning.

As a boss in a 9-1-1 center, I have to somehow shed the cloak
of so much negativity and mistrust and morbid humor. I have to
represent all of the GOOD things in a 9-1-1 center. I don a coat of
positive reinforcement for my people. I knew it would weather all
kinds of political slings and arrows. I was formidable against all
odds when I met with my committees of fire dudes and paramedics.
I also knew that for everything I had ever learned as a dispatcher,
we were all still a part of one big team. In my eyes, public safety
was just that: Public Safety. We were all responsible for all of it
and we had to take care of each other while looking out for the
good of the many. So I learned a lot about taking charge, leading
the way, and empowering people. The changes were taking place

and people were stepping up and becoming educated and involved. We were communicating and doing a great job at it.

When it came to hiring we were on the mark as well. We were lucky enough to have three awesome candidates in the early spring of 2005. It looked as if they were all going to make it too. I would pass through the training room periodically when they were all going through the two weeks of orientation. I would slip them trinkets that had our county name on them like a stress ball or a pen when the training supervisor wasn't looking. I know how dry that first couple of weeks can be. It is very much about policies and procedures and rules and regulations and contract language. Sometimes when he wasn't looking, I would make faces behind his back to let the newbies know that even the boss has fun here. We were rockin' as a center. I know that each and every one of them rocked my world. I felt like the transition from assistant director to director was finally gelling and I had my game face on most of the time. I loved my job and I was ecstatic to be able to give back to my dispatchers, finally!

Then one night my life changed forever. November 23, 2005. The eve before Thanksgiving. This was a different kind of call during a Thanksgiving weekend. I shall never look at this holiday the same again. I never imagined the two-way beep of my Nextel phone changing my life. My dispatch supervisor two-way'ed me as he had done a few million times before. I always knew when he was working. It was always good and bad. It was good that he trusted to ask me silly questions, bad that it was usually about some radio problem and I would wind up having to go in to the center and fix something. This night was beyond bad.

Bee-deep.

"Yeah."

Bee-deep.

"Kel, Stacy was involved in a fatal accident on her way to work tonight."

"Oh my god, NO!"

I am sure there were more words in there. I just can't remember all of them. All I know is that on the one and a half miles it took me to get to my office, all I could think of was, "Maybe I was wrong, maybe someone else died and she was just involved in the accident somehow." My mind was racing. I was in charge. I was the boss. I am supposed to fix things. I am supposed to know all of the resources like they do but on a higher level. What the hell was I supposed to do? Who? What? Where? When? And most of all—WHY?

Stacy was twenty-three years young when she came to us. She was let go from another dispatch agency due to funding cuts. She looked at several options and chose us because we looked like we knew how to have fun and still do the job. She was amazing. She was fun, vibrant, exuberant, life-giving, and had a forever-smile pasted on her face. She was the epitome of a young person in love with life. She was an awesome dispatcher too. We hit the jackpot with her. Before coming to us, while on her vacation time, she had spotted a wanted felon (for kidnapping and murder) and followed his vehicle while reporting his plate to the authorities. She was still receiving awards and thanks for helping apprehend that bad guy well after that fateful night in November. Stacy would do little things and make it seem like they were the most important thing she could do for you. She received graciously. She accepted the pen and the stress ball as if they were bars of gold. Her eyes lit up and she smiled a smile that went all the way across her face. I knew when I gave the trinkets to her that she already had plans of how to use them for the most fun. Life was simply amazing around Stacy. She glowed and wouldn't let anyone on her shift have sad or down times. She would gently nudge them and smile that smile in order to lift a mood. Negativity simply wasn't an option for her. Life was too much fun.

So when I got to the center and saw her squad, her teammates, in a state of shock, I could barely breathe. I took one look at their faces and like baby birds in a nest reaching up to the mother bird, they were desperate. They wanted me to come in and change the outcome or at least rewind the past couple of hours. I don't know what I did or said first, but I know that I had to exit out the back door for a second and get my bearings. We had our systems in place. There was a message being sent out for critical emergency response for others to relieve the ones in the chair that night. I gathered them up in my office. I called the State 9-1-1 Administrator, who is also my dear friend, Harriet. I advised her of what had happened and she hugged me through the phone. Then she did what she does from her past dispatcher days; she took over. She reminded me of my responsibilities and my resources. Then she said to call her back if or when I needed her further. I thanked her and went to join my staff in my office. As I had first explained to Harriet, I didn't know what to do. I was at a loss. I was supposed to somehow protect them. After all, I was supposed to make sure they go home the same way they come in, right? Now here they sat in my office in a circle of chairs crying and hugging and in disbelief. We all cried, and then cried some more. A couple of the gals cried about an upcoming Christmas present. It dawned on me that Stacy's family would not have her around for Thanksgiving or Christmas. It all started to sink in with me that Stacy was really gone. I got my dispatch staff the assistance they needed. My assistant director and I stayed with them or took turns staying with them until they could get debriefing and have some official help. We all stayed in touch and in contact with each other for days on end after that.

The on-duty supervisor was relieved to go help make notification. Like the rest of the squad, he knew some of the family members and wanted to be there. This was a close-knit team of night shift young folks. They hung out. They knew a lot about each other and were as close as family, if not closer. I let him go on behalf of the department. I felt it was more critical for me to stay behind for the rest of the center and be there for the processes that needed to go forward. I made a lot of notifications. I was contacted by a lot of people. It was now officially Thanksgiving and I was not going home any time soon. Immediately, the staff came up with an idea of having a memorial garden instead of a plaque. They wanted a remembrance of her life and her joy and the living she exemplified every day. I mentioned the request to the County Controller as I made notification to him. He said he would work with me and see if we could make it happen. He was an awesome life ring to have during the whole event. It was good to have support.

I finally went home for a couple of hours' sleep after talking with the supervisor about the family coming in for a visit. They wanted to come in later that afternoon. They said the media wanted to meet them and they asked if they could do the interview in my office. I happened to know the reporter (the right reporters can help you) and assured them that it would be fine. I met with my reporter friend first privately and gave my account of what had happened. I then asked her to be especially kind to the family. I trusted her as I had built a rapport with her and gave her news pieces from time to time. She agreed and said she would do right by the family.

Before they arrived, I called my friend Cy. He was running for Sheriff. He was a county commissioner. More than all of that, he was a trusted confidant and friend. I knew after his thirty-plus years in public safety and education that he would be able to direct me. I called that Thanksgiving Day and asked if he was sitting down. He could tell by the tone in my voice that I needed him.

"Cy."

"Yes, Kelly, are you okay?"

"Cy, I have to tell you some bad news and I figure all of the commissioners will be notified soon. I wanted you to hear from me."

"What is it, Kelly?"

"Cy, my dispatcher Stacy, the new one, who was only twenty-three, was killed in a car crash last night."

I could hear his exhale as he sat down and I felt his heart hurt for me. He assured me that I was doing all of the right things. He stated that he knew I would get through this stronger and better for all dispatchers everywhere. He had a lot of faith and love for me in that moment. Truly a public safety brother.

"Cy, what do I do or say?"

"You will find the words, Kelly, and I will be there for you. I will be there every step of the way."

"Okay, Cy. I can't believe this has happened."

"Neither can I, but if anyone can survive and come through this as an example, you can do it. Just remember, I will only be a phone call away."

"Thanks, Cy. Happy Thanksgiving, or something." We both grinned a little.

When the family drove in I noticed right away that they appeared to have slept less than I did. There were four cars full of family members. They just kept coming. We all huddled into my office. Before they got settled and before anyone could do any more introducing, I pulled out my brown paper bag of stress balls. The one Stacy loved so much. I tossed one to everyone there. Their eyes lit up. They had some fun and the dad, George, started to catch his breath. "This is so like Stacy." He smiled at me. He asked me if the 9-1-1 folks would wear their 9-1-1 clothing to the funeral. I assured him that we would undoubtedly represent 9-1-1. He responded with, "Good, because Stacy loved 9-1-1 and I know that she would want to be buried in her 9-1-1 jacket."

Once again, my breath leapt from my chest and I could barely speak, much less breathe. I smiled at George and told him I agreed. With his tear-smudged cheeks he smiled back at me. I knew we would be friends for a very long time.

We bonded that Thanksgiving Day. I adopted a family I had never known before. Another extended family branch from my 9-1-1 family tree. I believe that this is what we are supposed to do for each other. Be there. So this is what I did. By Saturday the funeral and arrangements for the cemetery were pretty well set. I went to my basement to paint and work off some stress during some down time. I received another two-way call from my shift supervisor.

Bee-deep.

"Yeah."

"Are you sitting down, boss?"

I'm thinking, are you kidding me? Is this some kind of joke?

"I have to call and tell you that Cy died this morning of a massive heart attack. And Kel, the funeral is Tuesday. The same day as Stacy's."

I was at a loss. I could not imagine any more grief on top of the guilt I had for breaking his heart that Thursday. As a boss, a director, a public safety professional, the weight was overwhelming. The fact that I could not attend his funeral or have any part in it seemed a cruel joke. Where was that metro phone book when I needed one?

I did make it to Cy's visitation. I cursed him in the casket for bailing on me. His wife reminded me that he would still be with me. She was right. Cy was right. I did do the right thing for Stacy and her family. Cy proved to me that I had it in me and could do a very professional job. If I had doubts, I would ask myself, "What would Cy say?"

While I only knew Cy for a short time, he filled a void that I had had since the days of my trainers. He was a mentor and someone whom I could count on to teach me things that I never realized I didn't know yet. I was lucky to have known him. I felt a calm come over me as I hugged this widow who lost such an amazing husband and friend. I had seen them together many times and had marveled at their youthful devotion and friendship to each other. They were such the perfect couple. And here she was comforting me for him. If I had a phone book, I would have thrown it several city blocks away. Talk about a stressful time.

As the organization of Stacy's funeral went forward, including two visitations, I knew I was in deep when the funeral home director and I had each other's personal cell phone numbers. I asked for and received full honors for Stacy's burial. As an on-duty, active employee of our public safety team, our honor guard protected and served us during the entire process. They were there for the visitation as they guarded the casket and they led us to the cemetery and participated in the burial. Whatever Papa George wanted, he got. I made sure of it! When he asked for bagpipes, I had to rely on the public safety team in the city where Stacy lived and worked before coming to us. This is where I met Sgt. Willy. Sgt. Willy and I became fast friends. He and I worked many hours together with the funeral home director. Sgt. Willy actually did most of the behind-the-scenes planning. He arranged for so much of the processional, line-up, cemetery service and more. Sgt. Willy and I had to bury a friend together and we had never before met. Stacy had a way of bringing people together like that.

On that bitter cold Tuesday when we said good-bye to our Stacy, Sgt. Willy and I stood together outside watching the many police, fire, and ambulance vehicles line up. He got a call on his radio from his wife (also an officer) down the way alerting us to another vehicle that needed to be scooted up front. We looked at each other and looked down the street, and just as we said it together, his wife came over the air and said, "...And it's a wrecker!" Sure enough! Every entity, every jurisdiction, everything you could imagine was there, in line, paying respects to an awesome dispatcher; even a local wrecker company. We laughed and looked up together and just hugged. It had to be Stacy!

One of the things I have always known is that when you bury a police officer or firefighter, they get some kind of full regalia. That's what the honors are about. It is pomp and ceremony. It is tradition. Up until now, I had never seen anything like it for anyone unless you were an officer or a firefighter. Those are impressive funerals. I've always sat in the back behind the officers or firefighters. At this funeral, we were in front. There were dozens of 9-1-1 professionals who came from all over to pay their respects on that bitterly cold day. They just kept coming. At one point, I had misplaced my gloves. There was an assistant director, Lisa, who had a spare as all good dispatchers have plenty of resources. They came in handy! We filled up that little church. Behind us our brothers and sisters in uniform supported us and held us together.

Sgt. Willy had gone over the procedure with everyone on how

the casket would leave the church. He had positioned everyone while conferring with me as to the line-up. When the church was emptied, all of the dispatch members went first and lined the many stairs. On both sides of the stairs we had dispatchers from all over lined all the way down to where the officers stood. There were lines and lines of officers in all colors of uniforms and then our firefighter brothers and sisters. It was phenomenal to see down the stairs the length and breadth of the lines. As the family exited the church, they were clearly moved. They paused at the top of the stairs and saw how much their daughter meant to an entire community. They got to the end and stood down by the hearse as Stacy's casket was then ushered from the church. As the pall bearers carried her between us there wasn't a dry eye anywhere. Even the pall bearers in uniforms had tears streaming down their cheeks. It was so cold outside. Still it felt warm inside my heart. I don't know exactly when I realized it; Stacy was with us all that day. She was approving and joking and making fun of us. I know it.

I learned that being a boss comes with all kinds of duties. I never imagined burying one of my own. I would never wish it upon anyone else. I would not hesitate to be there for one so honored to be laid to rest that way. I do think we all did the right thing. Sgt. Willy was most amazing. I couldn't have gotten through it without him and Sgt. Jungel and the honor guard. Papa George got everything he asked for that day. He got the bagpipes, the ceremony, the twenty-one gun salute, the taps, the full salute to bid farewell to a 9-1-1 dispatcher. Someone asked me what was so special about Stacy that she was buried like an officer with full honors. I replied, "She was one of the team, the Public Safety team!" And if I can add, she was a true hero in my eyes. Her positive outlook on the job and her devotion to making things right for people went beyond her words of "I like to help people"; she lived it. I like to think she got a kick out of that funeral, especially the wrecker!

I still keep in touch with George. I love Stacy's family. They are a lot like the kind of family I would choose if I had to choose one for myself. We communicate regularly and they have a standing open invitation to visit the center any time. As well, they also bring flowers and butterfly houses to the memorial garden behind the center. We brought it to life. There we all were, dispatchers and Stacy's family digging in the dirt, planting bulbs and sowing seeds of life. It was a good way to have closure. It was a wonderful way to bring about winds of change.

Hope

I do love this job. I love this profession. From the days when I first started and learned how to handle the stress and the tough calls and even tougher training partners, I have loved every minute of it. I have enjoyed learning and realizing that there is so much beautiful change still coming to make this job even more cool.

About a week after we got through the funerals and I was starting to catch up slowly on emails and voice mails and budget stuff, I got a strange call from a friend who owns his wrecker business. He and his brother ran separate businesses and were a great deal of help to me in creating and maintaining our wrecker policy for our No Preference Wrecker Rotation list. No kidding. We really have a list that we maintain and rotate so that when an officer needs a wrecker, it is considered an emergency request and they drop other things to help us out first. It worked only disjointedly before Bob and I sat down and crafted a better way. He was the coolest guy when it came to running a business, having honor and a good name. He wasn't above bringing in ice cream bars to my dispatch staff on occasion either. Or on the holidays he made sure to get everyone in the center something special. He was just a great guy trying to do a good thing.

So when his brother Jeff called and told me that Bob's back pain wasn't going away and they admitted him to the hospital, I wondered what happened. Jeff and I kept in touch and I even saw Bob a couple of times before I left on my much-needed vacation that December. By the time I returned, Bob was failing fast and Jeff encouraged me to come say my good-byes. I couldn't believe my ears. I gathered up my fire chief from the venue where Bob runs his wrecker business because I knew that they were very close. I asked if he wanted to come with me to say good-bye. We did and Jeff was right. Bob's health was failing. He died a short time later.

When Jeff asked for my assistance in helping with some of the funeral procession and such, I felt like I had never left that role. Remember the wrecker at Stacy's funeral? While it wasn't one of Bob's (it would have been if it weren't for other circumstances that got in the way), it was what we did. We all do the job with and for each other. Bob recognized that. He knew how hard dispatchers had it sometimes. My dispatch staff knew the folks at his shop and how hard they worked to earn a decent living. So off I went to help with yet another funeral procession. Did we have fun with that one! There was no service at a cemetery, so the huge number of wreckers wanted to proceed in an orderly fashion back to Bob's company about twenty miles away. The officer in the lead car said we needed to stay tight together and everyone put on flashers since we wouldn't have the processional flags on the vehicles. I placed four or five cars in between a mammoth wrecker for the entire line. There had to be thirty or forty wreckers. They came from all different companies including Bob's and Jeff's shops.

So here we were riding through downtown busy streets and intersections, running red lights and staying sandwiched between these enormous wreckers with their strobe lights flashing. There were people stopped in parking lots standing outside their trucks with their baseball caps crossed over their hearts in a salute to Bob. I had to grin at what he and Stacy must be doing. Cy surely had to be smiling, too. It was a beautiful thing, to be sure. In the words of my fire chief, "Kelly, as you get older, more people die on you." I dread the day I have to attend his funeral with all of the regalia! It is the right thing to do. I guess you never get used to them. It is, after all, a big part of the job. We deal with death and dying and harm and injury all the time. As 9-1-1 directors, we research more means, more ways to get more information more quickly and efficiently processed by the dispatchers in order for them to dispatch the 9-1-1 call. It is about service and safety and everything in between.

So people will continue to move on. My years in the profession have shown me that once you are a part of the team, it gets in your blood. You never shake it when you read about or hear about a responder down. You (at least I do) ask yourself, "What about the dispatcher?" What were they hearing or doing to try to expedite help to those in need? As a dispatcher/telecommunicator/call-taker, you are always asking yourself, "What if?"

When I lost an officer, I asked, "What if?" When I lost Stacy, I asked, "What if?" When I lost Cy, I asked myself a very hard, "What if?" Then it dawned on me. The thing they gave so selflessly was themselves. They walked the walk, they talked the talk. They moved people to do the right thing. They inspired, motivated, and deeply enjoyed helping people. I remembered why I wanted to become a director. I wanted to HELP the dispatchers. I wanted to give back to the profession.

After a few tumultuous, awesome, inspiring years as a 9-1-1 director, I found my way. I found the way to give back. I see so many of my colleagues through the ranks missing out on life because they get so stuck in the job. They can't seem to rise above the negativity and the despair of all the wretchedness. I see how I was then and I learned how to rise above it. I learned about choices and choosing to have a different outlook. I realized that not everyone in the world was like those people I dealt with day in and day out. Cy knew this secret too. He lived to inspire others to do the right thing, for the right reason, at the right time. He would be my light along with Stacy and Bob.

I went to speak with my friend the County Controller. He knew my struggles and triumphs. He was there to answer my dumb questions and ask me the hard ones. He encouraged me to find the answers and grinned real big when I found them. We both grew up together, you could say. I advised him that I would be stepping aside and we needed to find a replacement. He was encouraging as well as insightful. He accepted my resignation tendered with a commitment to make sure it was as smooth as possible for my staff.

I have since started my own company. I now train, motivate, and speak to 9-1-1 professionals all over the United States and Canada. I get to fill in the gaps for dispatchers everywhere. I can be like Cy and Stacy and inspire others to live a better life. I have the tools to train them to do just that. As I prepare for more classes, more training, more standards, I am learning what the standards are across the nation. There are vast differences in how dispatchers, telecommunicators, call-takers, and the rest are trained. There are even greater differences in their duties, expectations, and pay. When one looks at creating a national standard like there is in place for police officers and firefighters, the model is there. We only have to reach out and make it happen. It will be difficult at first. Knowing what I know about the size and make-up of all kinds of centers, there will be some challenges. Let's look at them as true learning challenges instead of obstacles. Let us raise the bar and set our sights on creating the professional credentials necessary to be the first, first responder. If we do not get involved in helping set the standards, who will? How will they know? Would they work universally? Isn't saving lives pretty universal?

I love this profession. I continue to challenge myself in learning what changes are coming that we must meet head on. There are new opportunities ahead, as we have learned from Hurricane Katrina. Telecommunicator Emergency Response Task force (TERT) is a team of telecommunicators that know and understand certain systems and programs at each other's centers so we can pick up and respond to help. This is definitely another huge step for dispatch when you think of it in terms of mutual aid, and the police and fire communities have been doing it for forever. The national organizations of NENA (National Emergency Number Association) and APCO (Association of Public Safety

Communications Officials) have partnered up to make TERT successful. We need to be able to help each other. If not us, then who will step up?

When Stacy died and everyone wanted to go to the funeral, there were a few who stayed back to man the center. What if we had TERT in Michigan and could have had people come in and know our systems and help us out for a few hours? In this day and age of interoperability and homeland security, who knows best how to communicate and think about the ins and outs of security? Dispatchers! Every day we take millions of phone calls across the globe answering the calls of "suspicious" nature. Who will be able to put it together that it is a terror plot, or a bio-chemical spill, or a mass destruction weapon? The dispatchers. Who do you think takes those calls of the suspicious incident to begin with and sorts it all out for the responders to get there safely and assess the scene safety? The dispatchers. There is plenty more coming to this wacky, crazed, mixed-up world of ours. We have a team of professionals in place waiting and wanting more training and more recognition for being the first ones on the scene to investigate. What remarkable resources these 9-1-1 professionals are.

We are lucky enough to live in a time when technology is affording us all kinds of communication abilities. We must remember to keep the telecommunicators current on that technology and those communication practices. There are places where people can and do call 9-1-1 from their Internet-connected phone through their computer and it routes to the last known address they entered into the computer. So, if they left their home in Michigan and called 9-1-1 from Texas to report a larceny, where, or better yet, who, do you think will answer that call? Another example: a person from Bangladesh is in downtown Detroit and does the same thing. If the 9-1-1 call goes to Bangladesh, how will the telecommunicators know who to transfer the call to back in Detroit? This technology is posing challenges today. What other technology is coming in the future? We need to think outside of the box and I ask them to stretch and learn with me. As a boss, I never had enough time to teach them all of the things coming their way in the warp speed it is coming at them and us. So now I can, in classes and seminars and at conferences. It is a good thing.

There are very few people who really get what we do when we answer that call. I applaud Senator Burns and Senator Clinton (now Secretary of State Clinton) for trying to make a difference and bring our issues to the forefront. There is an enormous need to bring 9-1-1 centers and all PSAPs (Public Safety Answering Points) up to certain technological standards to continue to answer the call. When the students at Virginia Tech asked why they couldn't text 9-1-1 with information, did it fall on deaf ears? The answer is no. NENA and APCO are making magnificent strides in seeking funding, moving legislation, and setting standards. We will get there because of the folks who work in their ranks. I also applaud the National Association of State Nine-One-One Administrators (NASNA) for setting the bar high and helping us to reach those standards.

In the end, it will be up to us to answer the call for us. We are all one team and we must stand up for each other. If we do not, then who will? I look forward to my path of renewed enlightenment and opportunity to train and inspire. I promise this much; I will do whatever I can do to give back to the profession that gave me my identity, my sense of what is right, and that perfect dose of humility to always keep me grounded. After all, it is no longer a local number for this butthead!

Look for Kelly's upcoming seminars
every April and October.

www.TheDoctor911.com